SACRED PLACES, SACRED TEACHINGS

༈ །གནས་ཆེན་ཆུ་སྲུ་ཁྱབ་པའི་གཙུག་ཁྲིམ།

His Eminence D. K. Garchen Rinpoche

༄༅། །འདུལ་འཛིན་དྲམ་པ་གཉན་ཆེན་རིན་པོ་ཆེ་དགོན་མཆོག་རྒྱལ་མཚན་ནས་གསར་
དུ་བྲིས་གནང་བའི་ Sacred Places, Sacred Teachings ཞེས་པའི་དཔེ་དེབ་ཞིག་
Wisdom Publications ཀྱིས་དཔར་སྐྲུན་བྱས་འདུག་པ་ལ་རྗེས་སུ་ཡི་རང་ཡོད།
གཉན་ཆེན་བོད་ནི་ནུད་དོན་རིག་པའི་གཞས་དབང་ཚམ་དུ་མ་ཟད། ཕར་ཕུལ་གནན་
དེང་རིག་གནས་གང་སར་མཁྲིན་སྐྱེན་མཆོག་ཏུ་ཡངས་པ་ཚན་ཞིག་ཡིན་པས་དེབ་
འདིས་སློག་པ་པོ་མང་པོར་ཕན་ཐོག་རྒྱ་ཆེན་འབྱུང་བའི་ཡིད་ཆེས་ཡོད་ལ། དེ་དེ་
བཞིན་འབྱུང་བའི་རེ་སྨོན་བཅས།

མགར་ཆེན་མིང་འཛིན་པ་དགོན་མཆོག་རྒྱལ་མཚན་ནས།
སྤྱི་ལོ་ ༢༠༡༥ ཟླ་ ༦ ཚེས་ ༦ ལ།

ཞ་བར་ཞིག་ཆེ་རྒྱུ་ལ་པ་དཀོན་ཁཞོ་ཞེག

His Eminence D. K. Garchen Rinpoche

I am delighted that Wisdom Publications has published this new book entitled *Sacred Places, Sacred Teachings*, written by the great Vinaya holder Khenchen Rinpoche Konchog Gyaltshen. I am confident that this book will be of great benefit to many readers, as Khenchen is not only a great scholar of Buddhist philosophy but also someone with exceptional insight into Eastern and Western cultures, ancient and contemporary.

I extend my heartfelt wishes for its success!

Garchen Konchog Gyaltsen
September 8, 2024

SACRED PLACES, SACRED TEACHINGS

Following the Footsteps of the Buddha

KHENCHEN
KONCHOG GYALTSHEN

Edited by Khenmo K. Trinlay Chödron

Foreword by His Holiness
Drikung Kyabgön Chetsang Rinpoche

Wisdom Publications
132 Perry Street
New York, NY 10014 USA
wisdom.org

Library of Congress Cataloging-in-Publication Data
Names: Konchog Gyaltsen, Khenchen, author. |
Trinlay Chödron, Khenmo, 1953– editor.
Title: Sacred places, sacred teachings: following in the footsteps of the Buddha /
Khenchen Konchog Gyaltshen, edited by Khenmo K. Trinlay Chödron; foreword by
His Holiness, Drikung Kyabgön Chetsang Rinpoche.
Description: New York, NY, USA: Wisdom Publications, [2025] |
Includes bibliographical references.
Identifiers: LCCN 2024032680 (print) | LCCN 2024032681 (ebook) |
ISBN 9781614299493 | ISBN 9781614299738 (ebook)
Subjects: LCSH: Buddh Gaya (India) | Sārnāth Site (India) |
Śrāvastī (Extinct city) | Spiritual life—Buddhism.
Classification: LCC BL2015.P45 K56 2025 (print) | LCC BL2015.P45 (ebook) |
DDC 294.3/435—dc23/eng20241004
LC record available at https://lccn.loc.gov/2024032680
LC ebook record available at https://lccn.loc.gov/2024032681

ISBN 978-1-61429-949-3 ebook ISBN 978-1-61429-973-8

29 28 27 26 25   5 4 3 2 1

Cover design by Marc Whitaker. Interior design by Gopa & Ted2, Inc.
For illustration credits, see page 263.
Translation of the *Heart Sutra* by Thupten Jinpa © 2015 Tenzin Gyatso,
the Fourteenth Dalai Lama, reprinted with permission
from Wisdom Publications.

Printed on acid-free paper that meets the guidelines for permanence
and durability of the Production Guidelines for Book Longevity
of the Council on Library Resources.

Printed in the United States of America.

Please visit fscus.org.

Lord, formerly monks who had spent the Rains in various places
used to come to see the Tathagata,
and we used to welcome them
so that such well-trained monks might see you and pay
their respects.
But with the Lord's passing,
we shall no longer have a chance to do this.

Ananda, there are four places
the sight of which should arouse emotion in the faithful.
Which are they?
"Here the Tathagata was born" is the first.
"Here the Tathagata attained supreme enlightenment"
is the second."
"Here the Tathagata set in motion the Wheel of Dhamma"
is the third.
"Here the Tathagata attained the Nibbana-element without
remainder" is the fourth.

Ananda, faithful monks and nuns, male and female lay-followers
will visit those places.
And any who die while making the pilgrimage
to these shrines with a devout heart will,
at the breaking-up of the body after death,
be reborn in a heavenly world.
—Mahaparinibbana Sutra

Publisher's Acknowledgment

The publisher gratefully acknowledges the generous help of the Hershey Family Foundation in sponsoring the production of this book.

Contents

 ༄ །འབྲི་གུང་སྐྱབས་མགོན།། DRIKUNG KYABGÖN

Foreword

IN THE 1980s, I tasked Khenchen Konchog Gyaltshen with establishing the first Drigung Kagyü center on the American continent. Since then, he has also taught inside Tibet and around the globe for decades.

In November 2011, Khenchen Rinpoche led over ninety pilgrims from various countries on a two-week pilgrimage to sacred Buddhist sites in India. During this journey, he imparted valuable teachings accessible to both beginners and advanced practitioners. In Bodh Gaya, practitioners were taught the short guru yoga of Lord Jigten Sumgön. In Sarnath, Varanasi, where the Buddha first turned the wheel of Dharma, Khenchen Rinpoche taught the four noble truths. At Vulture Peak, where Buddha turned the wheel of Dharma for a second time, Khenchen Rinpoche imparted teachings on the perfection of wisdom through the *Heart Sutra*. At Nalanda University, he shared the life stories of Shantideva and his classic work, the *Bodhicharyavatara*. In Kushinagar, he emphasized the importance of bodhichitta. In Lumbini, he introduced the practice of the fivefold path of *mahamudra*.

It is my sincere hope that this book will guide readers toward an authentic understanding of the Buddha's teachings and assist all sentient beings in their journey toward enlightenment.

With my prayers,

Drikung Kyabgön Tinle Lhundup
May 10, 2024
Kyoto, Japan

Preface

THIS SMALL BOOK is a collection of teachings that were primarily given during a pilgrimage to the four main Buddhist holy places in India and some of the secondary sites a decade ago. Originally, this trip was to be led by His Holiness Drikung Kyabgön Chetsang Rinpoche, who had agreed to give teachings along the way to whoever could participate. When His Holiness became ill shortly before the pilgrimage was to commence, with close to ninety participants joining from around the world, I was asked to lead the pilgrimage. It was a privilege to have such a great opportunity to receive blessings at these holy places. I was especially pleased about the teachings I could give, which became the core of this book. We were reminded of how these places came to be holy and remembered for thousands of years.

As the group progressed on its pilgrimage, I gave teachings that were inspired by the enlightened activities of the Buddha that took place at each stop. For example, we investigated the four noble truths at the place where the Buddha first taught them, and discussed the *Heart Sutra* where he first taught it to a vast assembly of humans, deities, and bodhisattvas. Many, many great scholars walked the paths at Nalanda, so I chose to highlight one of them, Shantideva, while we were there. While we can all aspire to see these sites in person, such travel may not be possible for everyone. To give you a sense of being there, each chapter begins with a description of what you would see if you were able to travel there. This is followed by an explanation of why each place is sacred and a bit of the history of what happened there. Reading teachings that were inspired by the holy sites of the Buddha's lifetime can inspire us in our own journey to liberation and enlightenment, right from our own home.

Since everything is interdependent, it took many contributors to materialize this small book. Zabrina Leung from Sweden recorded all the talks during the pilgrimage and took hours to transcribe them. She repeatedly encouraged me to turn the collection of talks into a book. I was traveling a lot, and had no time or energy to do it. Zabrina took the initiative to find other people who could help. Kay Candler did some editing, which I appreciate. Finally, the project was turned over to Khenmo Trinlay, who polished the English and went through the manuscript with me several times to improve its clarity and add some explanations. I am grateful to all these individuals. Without their sincerity, devotion to the precious Dharma teachings, the wisdom of the Buddha, this book would not have been accomplished.

To aid readers who are unfamiliar with Tibetan Buddhism, we included a glossary that contains short definitions of specialized terminology and identifies the persons mentioned in the book. As a quick reference, there is also a glossary containing the many enumerated lists that are so typical of Buddhist writings. Finally, there is an annotated bibliography of the writings mentioned that you may find useful as you pursue further study. Translations in this book are my own, unless otherwise cited in a note or the bibliography.

This book is dedicated to the welfare of sentient beings. I sincerely hope it will help many people to understand the Dharma, the wisdom and compassion of the Buddha. I want to remind anyone who reads this book: Don't just look at the words. Try to understand them and apply them in your life to get their full benefit. When we study and practice the precious Dharma, we need a perspective that encompasses more than this life or just oneself. Instead, we focus on a solution that results in complete perfection of the optimal goal for everyone.

Introduction

A PILGRIMAGE IS UNLIKE any other form of travel, and certainly any other activity from our daily life. If we recognize this from the start and appreciate our journey as a way not only to trace the Buddha's life, but also to appreciate how beings have benefitted from his activities, then a pilgrimage becomes so joyous. The Buddha uncovered the causes of suffering, revealed our innate mental clarity, and taught us how to gather the positive causes that lead to permanent happiness. These truths are universal. Of course, it is not easy to dispel the delusions that cause suffering; we have been habituated in them for a long time. So long, in fact, that we have come to believe our delusions are real. So we repeat the same mistakes over and over, and suffering never comes to an end. Everyone in the world strives for happiness their whole life, but in the end, no one is entirely free of suffering. The Buddha's wisdom pinpointed the root cause of our delusion for us and showed how lost we are in the jungle of confusion. The possibility of enlightenment gives us great hope and joy that suffering can actually end.

Pilgrims don't travel as tourists do, taking pictures and sightseeing, just looking a place over and quickly leaving for the next one. At each place we can reflect on the Buddha's wisdom and take the opportunity to appreciate how precious his teachings are now and have been for centuries. Through the ages, people from all over the world have sacrificed their time and resources to visit these holy places to honor the Buddha and his followers, and to receive blessings. Just as in ancient times, today people stay for days to study the precious Dharma. Afterward, they take the Buddha's message of wisdom, compassion, and purification back to their own countries. In this way, the Dharma has benefitted countless sentient beings all over the world since the Buddha transmitted it 2,600 years ago. How amazing!

Outwardly, these sites became holy because the Buddha blessed them by performing his enlightened activities there. Honoring these places today supports our efforts to build inner courage, wisdom, and compassion; to purify all our shortcomings; and to create peace and harmony within. When we become holy through the practice of the Buddha's instructions, then the places we go will be made holy. Think of Milarepa: even though he committed such harmful acts in his youth, now, every place he went during his lifetime is full of blessings because he became enlightened. This thought can encourage us to study and practice tirelessly.

The most important practices that the Buddha taught are love, compassion, bodhichitta, and causality. The Dharma is not just an academic philosophy, but is a practical method that dispels the confusion and mental afflictions that directly cause all the suffering in the world. When you encounter conflicts and obstacles, step back and reflect on these practices instead of indulging in the conflict. This will help to reduce pride and ego, and increase your understanding of others, allowing you to walk in others' shoes. Then through this wisdom and the method of compassion, a real sense of serenity is possible. We can't leave the teachings on the table and expect peace and happiness to come without effort. The Buddha gave complete instructions. Recalling interdependence, our part is to take responsibility for our study and practice.

All Buddhists are not buddhas; we are not all enlightened, so there is always a possibility we may make mistakes and face limitations. But as we progress in these practices, we will become happier and more peaceful. Then we will have the inner resources to help others. Bodhichitta is the consummate path and method to train our mind. Once our mind becomes a friend, we, too, become holy.

Interdependent arising is a fundamental doctrine held by all Buddhist traditions. It explains that no phenomena, including ourselves, exist inherently or as independent entities; everything arises in dependence on various causes and conditions. Our planet and all its inhabitants function within that framework. This is not just Buddhist philosophy; this is how all phenomena function, universally. We just need incisive awareness, a clear mind, to capture the reality nature of all phenomena. We cannot presume we know how reality works or guess at it. We have to measure our actions very carefully and create the right causes for what we desire.

After practicing relative bodhichitta, we practice ultimate bodhichitta or mahamudra. When the Buddha became enlightened, he declared, "I have found an unafflicted nectar that is deeply profound, total peace, free from fabrication, luminous, and unconditioned." This describes the nature of mind; every individual has it equally. The Buddha completely eliminated all delusion and directly realized absolute wisdom. That is the holiest among the holy.

Even though we have the potential to realize the nature of mind, it is like gold hidden in ore, or butter yet to be churned from milk. With great compassion, the Buddha showed the method to reveal our true nature, the universal way every being is constituted. We all want to be free from suffering and always desire peace and happiness, but we remain ignorant of how to accomplish this. Everyone, even small ants, keeps busy looking for a better place, a place with less suffering. We dedicate our entire lives to this endeavor, but the day never comes when we can say, "Now my mission is accomplished." We are always dissatisfied; we never have enough. Even if someone made a billion dollars, they would still be hungry for more. The Buddha discovered total satisfaction, the ultimate achievement, and left instructions on how we, too, can achieve the same. We already have this great path; we don't have to research anything, just follow it. That's why I called this book *Sacred Places, Sacred Teachings: Following the Footsteps of the Buddha.*

Mara, you should not toil to no purpose;
give up your murderous intent and go in peace.
For this sage can no more be shaken by you
than Meru, the greatest of mountains, by the wind.

Fire might lose its nature of being hot,
water its liquidity, earth its solidity,
but in view of the meritorious deeds accumulated by him
through many ages he cannot abandon his resolution.

For such is his vow, his energy, his mental power, his compassion
    for all,
that he will not rise up till he has attained the truth,
just as the thousand-rayed sun
does not rise without dispelling the darkness.

As by rubbing wood long enough a man obtains fire,
and by digging the earth deep enough he obtains water;
nothing is impossible of achievement to the man of perseverance.
Everything that is undertaken by the proper method
is thereby necessarily carried out with success.

Therefore, since the great physician,
in his pity for the world lying distressed in the diseases of passion, etc.,
toils for the medicine of knowledge,
he should not be hindered. [. . .]

For today is the appointed time
for the ripening of those deeds
which he has done in the past for the sake of illumination.
Thus, he is seated in this place exactly like the previous sages.

For this is the navel of the earth's surface,
entirely possessed of the highest power;
for there is no other spot in earth
that can bear the force of his concentrated thought.
—Ashvagosha, *Buddhacarita*

CHAPTER 1

Bodh Gaya: The Buddha's Enlightenment

IN BUDDHIST COSMOLOGY, Bodh Gaya is the strongest, most stable place on earth, the only place that could have supported the Buddha at the moment of enlightenment. It is marked by the Mahabodhi Temple, an imposing tower built and rebuilt on the same spot for millennia. The structure that you see today is a reconstruction begun by Burmese patrons and continued by the British in the 1800s. Improvements continue constantly, such as the addition of a marble circumambulation path and restoration of a railing said to have originated with Nagarjuna in the second century CE. Inside the temple is a statue of the Buddha at the moment of awakening that dates to the tenth century. On the side opposite the temple entrance is a large, old tree. It is not the original Bodhi Tree that the Buddha sat under; that one became quite deteriorated and blew over in a storm in 1876. In the third century BCE, King Ashoka's daughter had taken a cutting from the original tree to Sri Lanka, where it survives. When the tree at Bodh Gaya died, a cutting from the Sri Lankan tree was returned and grew into the one we see today. But some say that today's tree spontaneously regenerated out of the original roots.

7

Siddhartha's Journey to Bodh Gaya

Before his enlightenment, Siddhartha had been engaged in
ascetic practices for some time, and his body had grown weak.
After regaining his strength from a meal of milk and rice
offered by a local girl named Sujata (see chapter 7), Siddhartha walked on to Bodh Gaya and seated himself beneath a fig
tree on what became known as the *vajrasana*, or adamantine
seat. He knew now that a Middle Path between extreme asceticism and self-indulgence must be traversed. He resolved not
to leave that seat until he found final enlightenment, no matter what might happen to his physical form. Thus he began his
final meditations in the place where all buddhas awaken.

Mara came to prevent Siddhartha's enlightenment in every
way that he could. He sent his daughters to tempt the bodhisattva with lust, sent murderous armies to attack, and offered
to make him ruler of the world, but nothing disturbed Siddhartha's meditation. Finally, Mara claimed that the seat of enlightenment was his own. Mara's demons bore witness to his
claim and taunted the buddha-to-be by asking where his own
witnesses were. Siddhartha silently reached his right hand out
to touch the ground, and the earth itself affirmed that he was
the *Tathagata*. Throughout the night, he continued in deep
meditation. He acquired the three knowledges: knowledge of
past lives, his own and all other beings; knowledge of the operation of *karma*, or cause and effect; and knowledge that he was
truly and completely free of all obscurations and obstacles,
that he had pierced through to the ultimate nature of reality.
He meditated without further interruption until the last veils
of ignorance were cleared away and he attained the *vajra*-like
absorption of buddhahood. At dawn, he proclaimed:

Through many a birth I wandered in samsara,
seeking, but not finding, the builder of the house.
Sorrowful is it to be born again and again.
O house-builder! You are seen.
You shall build no house again.
All your rafters are broken. Your ridgepole is shattered.
My mind has attained the unconditioned.
Achieved is the end of craving.[1]

Bodh Gaya is where a prince became the Teacher, where a simple monk became the World Honored One, where one man became the founder of one of the world's great religions. It is where Prince Siddhartha purified all the gross and subtle obscurations and directly perceived the unfabricated, uncontrived reality of phenomena. From then on, he was called the Buddha, the Fully Awakened One. There are so many religions in this world; it seems almost every country has a different one. Some traditions are more philosophical, where others emphasize practice or devotion. You can describe Buddhism as either a philosophy or a religion, but at its core it is the explanation of the nature of reality, which the Buddha realized at his awakening under the Bodhi Tree.

The one we know as the historical buddha, Shakyamuni, was born as Prince Siddhartha, the son of the powerful king Shuddhodana, in the Himalayan mountains. He was brought up in a special way to make him physically and mentally fit to be king. He was taught by the best teachers and given every opportunity to attain all the knowledge that existed at that time. His early life was spent entirely within a well-guarded, luxurious palace. He remained there until he was twenty-nine, when he left the palace to visit the kingdom and learn about the lives of common people. It was then that he actually learned the reality of samsara. It was immediately obvious to him that not everyone lived in the luxury he was accustomed to. He encountered poor, uneducated, sick, old, and dying people for the first time.

He saw that they worked hard as farmers or businessmen, that they faced many types of physical suffering and all sorts of predicaments, and that people are victims of mental afflictions, too. These sights caused the prince to think seriously about how to help his subjects. He felt a sincere responsibility to them, and was not at all attached to his power, authority, fame, and wealth. When his father noticed this, he feared that the prince might leave the kingdom permanently. He arranged for the prince to take a wife, Yashodhara, in the hope that attachment to her would make him stay. But instead of ascending to the throne, the prince renounced the kingdom and left to search for a way to end the suffering he'd witnessed.

Over the course of the next six years, Siddhartha met many teachers who were famous for their scholarship and meditation practice. He received their teachings, and he exercised his mind by contemplating and meditating according to their instructions. From an extremely luxurious life, he undertook drastic asceticism, even going without food for long periods. Although he achieved a very high state of meditation called the space-like absorption, he felt that there was still more he could achieve. It was then that he arrived in Bodh Gaya and sat under the Bodhi Tree to meditate. With complete dedication and determination, he vowed, "Even if my body disintegrates, I will remain until I achieve the final goal." Because of his determination and one-pointed mind, he was able to reveal the nature of the universe; he penetrated to the core of reality and uncovered the universal nature of the mind. Everything about the constitution of reality, the whole of phenomena, was precise and clear. This unfabricated wisdom was accompanied by perfect compassion, which means that all of his obscurations and delusions had totally vanished. From that time on, he was called the Buddha, the Fully Awakened One. To distinguish him from other buddhas, we also know him as Buddha Shakyamuni, with "Shakya" being his family or clan's name and "muni" being the Sanskrit word for sage.

This world is permeated by afflicted confusion and suffering—we can all agree on that. Beings suffer from aging, sickness, and dying. They suffer from not getting what they want and from getting what they do not want. For the most part, we have enough food, clothing, and a place to live. But instead of enjoying these good conditions, we create problems for ourselves and others by engaging in confusion, hatred, and greed. These problems cannot be solved by laws and rules, or by becoming wealthier. We need wisdom and compassion to do that, as well as the skill to handle mental confusion. We spend our whole lives chasing happiness and avoiding suffering, to no avail.

All phenomena of samsara and nirvana are constituted within the framework of causality. This reality is not experienced just by Buddhists, but rather by every sentient being in the world, human and nonhuman. But from that starting point, there are many different ways to approach and solve this problem of suffering. In fact, because sentient beings have differing levels of mental capacity and different ways of thinking, there are said to be 84,000 types of mental affliction. The

Buddha taught ways to comprehend and purify each one of these delusions through what are called the 84,000 heaps of Dharma teachings.

The approach in the Buddha's teachings is not one of blind faith. Rather, we are taught to examine things for ourselves and find solutions to our problems. The Buddha is not a creator of virtue and nonvirtue; rather, he is the guide who shows the path to the end of suffering. He is a teacher who can point out the best direction, but we must travel the path ourselves. We are our own masters. He taught that there are four reliable guideposts. We should make sure that we contemplate them and understand their meaning.

1. Rely on the teaching, not the teacher. Take refuge in the teachings of wisdom and compassion; study and practice them. Having a teacher with a pleasing personality is not as important as the teachings they give.

2. Rely on the ultimate teachings about emptiness and nonduality, not the relative ones. Conventional or relative phenomena are impermanent. As we progress on the path we will have to leave the relative teachings behind. Take the ten *bhumis*, or stages on the path to enlightenment, as an example. When we arrive at a new level, we must leave the preceding stage behind.

3. Rely on the meaning, not the words. Don't be attached to beautiful words, but contemplate the meaning of the precious Dharma.

4. Rely on wisdom, not mundane consciousness. Wisdom is knowing the unfabricated nature of reality as it is. Consciousness is ever-changing mental activity.

Modern scientists pose questions and, on the basis of their various investigations, find solutions. We appreciate their methods, especially those of quantum physics, because the Buddha's teaching operates in much the same way. Only it can go farther because it examines the mind. Because the mind is not material, it cannot be found through any machine or medical device, no matter how far modern technology advances. Scientists may be able to examine the brain in great detail, but not consciousness itself. Communication, transportation, the internet, computers, and so forth are indeed very sophisticated, yet they cannot discover the nature of reality. The nature of reality simply cannot be found through the physical methods researchers rely on; it can only be revealed by the consciousness within us. Although close at hand, the mind remains mysterious to us. The Buddha perceived the nature of reality fully and directly, so that nothing was hidden from him. This is what we mean by *buddha*: a fully awakened mind that knows everything and sees everything clearly.

The Buddha's Realization

When the Buddha attained buddhahood, he said that he had found an unafflicted nectar that is deeply profound, total peace, free from fabrication, luminous, and unconditioned. That *deeply profound* thing he found is the mind. Mind is infinite and complex. Mind neither exists nor does not exist. You cannot pinpoint its location, its form, its color, or weight, so from this perspective, it does not exist. Yet it is the foundation of all we experience in samsara and nirvana. Conceptual thoughts manifest without cessation within the sphere of the mind. When we realize its nature, it is nirvana. When we do not realize its nature, we are ignorant and confused in samsara, trapped in the duality of hope and fear.

All the modern technologies that we have now are creations of the mind. It appears that there is no end to what the mind can imagine, both positively and negatively. Thus, samsara is endless because of the mind, but nirvana is infinite as well. The achievements of *shravakas, pratyekabuddhas*, bodhisattvas, and, ultimately, buddhas are also states of mind. For us, with unenlightened minds, it is not easy to comprehend the real nature of mind.

The Buddha further described his realization as *total peace*. In samsara, all our difficulties arise from the confused mind and are based on the dual nature of hope and fear. Conflicts—whether they are within oneself, between individuals, within a country, or between nations—manifest out of confusion that is based in ignorance. This confusion also allows attachment, anger, pride, jealousy, greed, and so forth to arise. Thus, it is through confusion that we create suffering. We are led to chase after the causes of suffering as if they were our friends. We destroy the possibilities for peace and happiness as if they were our enemies. This is how the suffering of samsara is created by everyone in the world, not just by Buddhists. On the other hand, when we look inward, contemplate, and relax, there is great peace and joy, even before buddhahood is achieved. Buddhahood, complete enlightenment, brings absolute, unafflicted peace because all mental delusion and confusion have been dispelled, and ignorance has become wisdom. That is what the Buddha realized and is what we are seeking to achieve by following the path he created.

The Buddha said that the nature of mind is *free from fabrication*. This means that everything is interdependent, interconnected; nothing stands independently. All the phenomena outside ourselves, both animate and inanimate, and everything inside ourselves—especially the self—are all interdependent, interconnected, and interrelated manifestations of the mind. Nothing can manifest without causes and conditions. When you carefully examine the appearance of anything, whether material, physical, or mental, you can understand that nothing exists independently. Take a simple cup of tea as an example. Someone planted and cultivated the tea plant; the sun shone and rain fell to make the plant grow; someone else harvested it; the leaves were dried, packaged, transported, and sold. In your kitchen, you heated water, found a cup, and made tea. At each of these steps, there were hundreds of other supporting causes and conditions all playing a role in interdependence.

Appearances are elaborations on emptiness that manifest only because of causes and conditions. This lack of independent existence is called emptiness free of elaboration. This is the puzzle that has to be examined carefully and solved.

All phenomena manifest within that very emptiness; phenomena and emptiness are indivisible. In modern times, quantum physicists have come to much the same conclusion. Emptiness is without edges, without limits, without center, without boundaries, selfless—completely free of any kind of elaboration. The Buddha realized this directly, which brought his confusion to an end, and then he taught the laws of causality on that basis. Because he revealed the truth of reality itself, we cannot say that this truth is limited to Buddhists. It is a description of every being's reality.

But the Buddha also said that the nature of the mind is not merely empty, it is *luminous* effulgence. The luminous mind is clear and precise, inseparable from emptiness. The Buddha has two types of wisdom: the wisdom of knowing reality as it is and the wisdom of knowing everything. Knowing reality as it is means cognizance of all manifestations and their chains of causality. Within the context of emptiness, all phenomena of samsara and nirvana are of one taste, that of emptiness, and are free of elaboration. The wisdom of knowing everything means understanding that all the various physical and mental manifestations are constituted within the framework of causality. In the state of enlightenment, the Buddha captured this directly and clearly without any judgment. This vast scope of knowledge comes from the practice of calm abiding meditation accompanied by critical insight—not from machines. In samsara, every individual has infinite chains of causality— that is, chains of causes and results. In enlightenment, in the state of nirvana, there are also infinite causes and conditions. Without any judgment, the Buddha saw everything, and he perceived it all directly and clearly. This is what the Buddha attained, and is also our ultimate goal.

Finally, the Buddha said that the nature of reality, including the nature of the mind, is *unconditioned*. Because the very nature of self is empty, it is thus indivisible—so the nature of the self is said to be uncompounded. Birth itself is unproduced; as the *Heart Sutra* says, "Form is emptiness, and emptiness is form. Form is no other than emptiness, and emptiness is also no other than form." That is what is meant by "unconditioned." *Dharmakaya*, the very nature of our mind, is also described as being uncompounded. By combining wisdom and method, we can free ourselves from all types of suffering; investigation followed by conviction allows us to first understand the functioning of reality and then to put that understanding into our meditation practice. This helps us purify our mental afflictions because when we destroy the cause (ignorance) there can be no result (affliction and suffering).

Through meditation practice, we, too, can realize and capture what the Buddha described as the profundity of the mind, which is completely peaceful, free from elaboration, luminous, and uncompounded. When one's meditation in the equipoise state has these qualities, delusions and mental afflictions dissolve. There is no other place for them to go. Everything is just a manifestation, and every manifestation dissolves into that state like a bubble dissolving into water or a cloud dissipating into the sky without a trace. That is why the Buddha could say, "I have attained buddhahood. I have achieved these qualities. Now I know samsara and nirvana." That is the enlightenment that the Buddha attained in the place called Bodh Gaya. It is the whole purpose of our efforts in studying and practicing the Dharma: to end our confusion and free ourselves from the layers of suffering.

The great seer understood that the factors [of causation]
are suppressed by the complete absence of ignorance.
Therefore, he knew properly what was to be known
and stood out before the world as the Buddha.

The best of men saw no self anywhere from the summit of
    existence downwards
and came to tranquility, like a fire whose fuel is burnt out,
by the eightfold path of supreme insight,
which starts forth and quickly reaches the desired point.

Then as his being was perfected, the thought arose to him,
"I have obtained this perfect path which was traveled
for the sake of the ultimate reality
by former families of great seers, who knew the higher and
    the lower things."

At that moment of the fourth watch when the dawn came up
and all that moves or moves not was stilled,
the great seer reached the stage which knows no alteration,
the sovereign leader, the state of omniscience.

When, as the Buddha, he knew this truth,
the earth swayed like a woman drunken with wine,
the quarters shone bright with crowds of siddhas,
and mighty drums resounded in the sky.
—Ashvagosha, *Buddhacarita*

CHAPTER 2

Bodh Gaya: Refuge

MONUMENTS associated with the time immediately after the Buddha's enlightenment surround the Mahabodhi Temple in Bodh Gaya. For the first week after he awakened, the Buddha remained seated on the *vajrasana*, the "adamantine seat" mentioned in the previous chapter. During the second week, he gazed in concentration at the Bodhi Tree. This is commemorated by the Animesha Lochana Stupa near the entrance. For the third week, he paced in walking meditation near the Bodhi Tree, a lotus blossom springing up with each step. A raised platform holding eighteen footprints within stylized lotuses in relief runs alongside the Mahabodhi Temple. There are ruins of a great many more temples, monasteries, and stupas on the grounds around the temple. For practitioners, different areas are set aside for prostration, meditation, and making offerings. Surrounding the temple grounds are many more beautiful temples and monasteries built by traditions from all over the world.

People travel to Bodh Gaya from all over the world to worship and say prayers. They sacrifice their time and resources to do so because they want to be free from suffering and to have peace and happiness. Therefore, we should have a good understanding of why we go on a pilgrimage or engage in any other practice for that matter. We should appreciate the opportunity, rejoice, and relax. Sometimes we will face discomfort and difficulty, but these things are temporary. Let go of them and keep the objective, enlightenment, in mind.

After his awakening, the Buddha contemplated whether he could teach his Dharma to others. He despaired of finding anyone who could understand the profound truth and the path to its realization. The deity Brahma appeared to him, and begged him to share what he knew, assuring him that there were some with just a small amount of dust covering their eyes, who were ready to receive his teachings. The Buddha looked out with eyes of compassion and saw that this was true, so he agreed to teach, starting in Sarnath. It was this act of becoming a teacher that spurred a lineage of teachers that has brought the Dharma to us today, and what makes him our refuge in samsara.

Refuge is a very important subject that we should take care to understand. Refuge is the gate that opens onto freedom from confusion, that leads from samsara to buddhahood. While we're in samsara, we don't have the precise and clear understanding to know which causes lead to peace and happiness, nor do we have the wisdom to understand the causes of suffering. We constantly make mistakes, so there is not a single day that is completely free of suffering. Even if we happen to be rich or famous or smart, even if we work hard and make countless sacrifices, in the end we live with disappointment. This is because, blinded by our ignorance, we take refuge in the wrong objects.

Everyone in samsara is bewildered by confusion, shrouded in ignorance. Everyone in the world wants peace and happiness—this will never change, no matter what you do or where you go. It is also obvious that suffering will not go away and that peace will not manifest just by wishing for it, talking about it, saying prayers, or chanting. To gain the desired result, we must create the proper causes and conditions. Thus, we need a teacher who can explain these causes and conditions clearly and precisely, and then we must follow his or her instructions on how to create them. It is the same with the leadership of a country. If the leader has a good, clear goal and explains to the people how to accomplish it, harmony and prosperity will result. On the other hand, if the leader is selfish, arrogant, or uneducated, he leads the country toward the wrong causes, and chaos results. This demonstrates that it is the causes that define the nature of the result. Universally, the right causes bring peace and happiness, and the wrong causes bring suffering.

Here, we are talking about the demarcation between samsara and nirvana. Nirvana, the state of enlightenment, has the nature of wisdom, compassion, and skillful means; all confusion has dissolved. The root cause of samsara is ignorance. That ignorance is the basis of our confusion, which in turn spawns all the afflictions, such as pride, jealousy, anger, greed, attachment, and so forth. As long as we stay within that dimension, suffering can never end. Thus, our real enemies are the afflicting emotions. Our focus must be to uproot these mental disturbances.

Consider a very intelligent scientist who creates a sophisticated weapon that can destroy millions of lives in a second. Without being smart, how could he create such a thing? He thinks he has accomplished a very great thing, a reason to be happy. But his intelligence did not bring about a genuine cause for peace and happiness—only a cause for more suffering. This is called afflicted intelligence. In contrast, the Buddha's wisdom is unafflicted. With critical insight, he correctly saw the operation of all causes and conditions and taught the wisdom known as the Dharma on that basis. Thus, he was able to explain exactly what causes suffering and what will free us from the vicious cycles of samsara. We should take refuge with full conviction in cause and effect and with a full understanding of what it means to be enlightened. Without that approach, Buddhism is reduced to cultural belief or habit instead of being a living path to freedom through universal truth.

We take refuge in the Buddha, Dharma, and Sangha. The Buddha is fully enlightened, one who purified all the obscurations, who vividly and precisely illuminated the perfect wisdom. The Dharma, the Buddha's teachings, encompasses both the mundane, relative truth and the ultimate truth known to the enlightened ones. Step by step, we utilize these two to reach our own awakening. Sangha refers to the ordinary people who have practiced successfully, and includes shravaka *arhats* and great bodhisattvas.

Buddha Shakyamuni, the person who achieved enlightenment in our age and who has undefiled compassion and wisdom, has been an inspiration for millions of people. But we should not let our concepts about this individual limit our idea of refuge. When we take refuge in the Buddha, we do not take refuge in just one individual being, like a specific statue or painting. We take refuge in the enlightenment of all the buddhas of the three times—past, present, and future. We do this to release the confusion and ignorance of samsara and turn toward wisdom and compassion. This is what the buddhas all do: they see the delusion and confusion of all sentient beings and how this leads them to suffer unnecessarily. With unlimited compassion, they teach the sacred Dharma, which is the collection of the buddhas' wisdom, the perfect path.

The Dharma teaches us how to achieve buddhahood. Right from the beginning, we should have the right understanding of why we are studying and practicing the Dharma. We practice to purify the causes of suffering, to turn from the wrong ways toward the right ways. Beings universally want peace and happiness; this fact is not just some cultural belief or tradition. Since that is the case, we must create the proper causes for peace and happiness. The unwanted circumstances that everyone in samsara encounters all result from the causes each being created. Our Dharma study allows us to identify the causes of suffering and peace. Thus, we take refuge in the Buddha, the state of enlightenment, and in the Dharma that teaches us how to achieve that state.

The Sangha that we take as an object of refuge consists of followers of the Buddha who studied and practiced the Dharma successfully. They are highly accomplished in their realization. They exemplify successful practice, and inspire us to follow the path ourselves. The term sangha can be used in various contexts to mean different things. In order to be considered an object of refuge, one must have dispelled confusion. While we don't take refuge in the ordinary sangha community of fellow practitioners, we do support each other. Within the religious community we must make every effort to achieve harmony by applying what we have learned.

The Buddha's teachings are not just for Buddhists, but for every sentient being. When we take refuge, we do not do so just for ourselves, but rather for all sentient beings. Thus, after we take refuge, we pray:

> May all mother sentient beings, boundless as the sky,
>   have happiness and the causes of happiness.
> May they be liberated from suffering and the causes of
>   suffering.
> May they never be separated from the happiness which is
>   free from sorrow.
> May they rest in equanimity, free from attachment and
>   aversion.

This attitude of expansiveness opens your heart and frees it from both attachment to and aversion toward sentient beings. We follow in the Buddha's footsteps steps joyfully with a feeling of privilege, recognizing that everyone has an opportunity to be so privileged.

Through this sort of practice, we will achieve the impartial mind, the mind of equanimity. Bodhichitta embraces every sentient being without judgment. There is no need to judge anyone. No matter what their situation, everyone equally wants peace and happiness, and everyone equally wants to be free from suffering. Practice that mind, the mind of space. Temporarily the rich become poor and poor become rich. Nothing is fixed.

Consider your usual mental state. What makes you unhappy? What brings you mental suffering? Why are you upset or angry? Why are you attached? Looking at these subjects gives you an opportunity to distinguish between confusion and wisdom. We take refuge in wisdom, the cause of peace and happiness, and leave behind confusion, which is the cause of suffering. We take refuge because we want peace and happiness and because we want to be free from suffering. This is what the Dharma is about. That is why we study and practice. So from this point of view, we all should rejoice: "I am so fortunate because I have this opportunity to study and practice the precious Dharma."

Take a deep breath and exhale all your tension. Visualize Buddha Shakyamuni as an embodiment of all buddhas, the Dharma, and the Sangha. Recall your desire to be free of the confusion of samsara and attain enlightenment for the benefit of all other sentient beings. With strong devotion, repeat three times, "I take refuge in you as the Buddha. I take refuge in you as the embodiment of the Dharma. I take refuge in you as the perfection of the Sangha." Then visualize the Buddha melting into light and dissolving into you from the crown of the head downward. Meditate that your body, speech, and mind are permeated with the Buddha's blessing, and that this purifies all your obscurations. The Buddha's body, speech, and mind become inseparable from your own in the nature of light. Then dissolve everything into emptiness, and meditate in the natural state of pervading emptiness. When you are finished, say dedication prayers. You can do this practice in the morning and evening. It is important to feel that your afflictions and mental disturbances are fully purified, and then maintain the nature of compassion and awareness throughout the day and night.

The people there at that time, perceiving His gravity and might
and His glorious form surpassing that of mankind,
were lost in amazement.

On seeing Him, whoever was going in another direction stood still;
whoever was standing in the road followed him;
whoever was going quickly went slowly,
and whoever was sitting down sprang up.

Some worshiped Him with joined hands,
others honored Him by saluting him with their heads,
others greeted Him with kindly words;
none passed on without doing him reverence.
—Ashvagosha, *Buddhacarita*

CHAPTER 3

Bodh Gaya: Guru Yoga

A PRINCE SAT down at Bodh Gaya and a buddha arose from that same seat. The great tree he sat under has died, temples erected to commemorate his accomplishments have fallen and been rebuilt, no trace is left of most of the monasteries that housed his followers, and the great libraries burned long ago. But the Dharma that the Buddha taught is just as fresh as it was 2,600 years ago. Students like ourselves are learning it from teachers who in turn had learned it from an unbroken chain of masters going back to the Buddha himself. This legacy is now being handed over to us. Our responsibility is to study and practice well so that chain remains unbroken.

Our purpose in studying and practicing the Dharma is not to become great scholars and write a lot of books, nor is it just a pastime or a hobby. We learn about suffering, causality, bodhichitta, emptiness, and the rest in order to become free from suffering. All our undesirable suffering originates in confusion based on ignorance. Confusion is a fabricated mindset that hides the innate nature of the mind. Thus, the main concern of our Dharma practice is to remove these fabrications and impediments. This is still possible in our present time because the teachings have not been lost or watered down over more than two millennia. The freshness and the blessings of the lineage have been passed down from the Buddha to one's root guru to you, the practitioner. The teachings are alive, so we can do more than just worship a statue, recite aspirational prayers, or recite mantras. We can unite our mind with the Buddha's mind and gain enlightenment ourselves by purifying our afflicting emotions and obscurations. This is the essential meaning of guru yoga practice: to unite your own mind with the guru's enlightened mind.

The Vajrayana system encompasses many skillful methods for transformation and purification of the mind. It has, for example, a great variety of meditation practices. Some take days to complete a single session and others take just a few minutes. Here, I will describe a very short guru yoga practice called *A Guru Yoga that Brings the Dharmakaya onto the Path*, the text for which can be found in appendix A. If you are rushed, it can be completed in ten or fifteen minutes. If you have enough time, the practice can be extended for hours. Although it is short, this practice contains vast and profound meaning.

Jigten Sumgön, Founder of the Drigung Kagyü

The "guru" in this guru yoga practice is Jigten Sumgön, a very important figure in Buddhist history who founded the Drigung Kagyü lineage of Tibetan Buddhism in the twelfth century. As a young man, he had the rare opportunity to learn reading and writing. Because of that and his good karma, he undertook vigorous study and practice without wasting his time. He met many excellent teachers from whom he learned general Buddhist philosophy, Vajrayana, and Mahamudra. He met his principal teacher, Phagmo Drupa, when he was twenty-five years old. Jigten Sumgön received all the teachings of the lineage that extended from the Buddha to Phagmo Drupa, and he put them into practice as much as he could. During the day he received teachings, and at night he went to his room to practice and contemplate what the teacher had taught. After his teacher passed away, Jigten Sumgön went into strict retreat for seven years and attained buddhahood when he was thirty-five years old. He destroyed the causes of samsara and fully revealed his inner qualities, just as the Buddha did in Bodh Gaya. At the time of his enlightenment, he sang:

I have realized the philosophy of interdependence.
I have completely revealed all the Vajrayana teachings.
I have found the treasure of Vajrayana teachings.
There is no gap between meditation and nonmeditation.
I am an enlightened yogi.[2]

Jigten Sumgön taught tirelessly until he was seventy-five years old, and over the course of his lifetime gathered hundreds of thousands disciples. Most of them studied and practiced and dedicated themselves to mountain retreat. Many were freed from samsara and achieved various levels of enlightenment. Jigten Sumgön's wisdom and compassion were as vast as space and pervade still every sentient being.

In his writings and teachings, Jigten Sumgön took care to communicate the Buddha's universal message. Many mistakenly believe that Buddhism is something that the Buddha invented. Jigten Sumgön was very clear in teaching that the Buddha simply revealed how every phenomenon of samsara and nirvana is constituted, how everything functions within the framework of causality. Whether one is a Buddhist or not, whether one is human or not, doesn't matter. Our actions are causes that will bring a related result. For example, killing someone becomes a cause that leads to great suffering later. As the saying goes, "What goes around, comes around." From this point of view, we can understand that the Buddha's message is for everyone. Jigten Sumgön also taught interdependence from the outer, inner, secret, and ultimate points of view. Included within these teachings are all the teachings of the sutra system and all four classes of tantra teachings. The important points of his teaching on these subjects, and many others, can be found in his text commonly called the *Gongchik* in Tibetan, or *One Thought*.

It is quite essential to know the qualities of one's root and lineage gurus, as well as their life and liberation stories, in order to make a connection with them. Many life stories of Jigten Sumgön were written by his disciples in Tibetan. A few have been translated and can be found in books such as *The Great Kagyu Masters* and *Scintillation of the Precious Vajra*. Life stories tell us how past masters studied and practiced the Buddha's teachings, how fully they developed their wisdom and compassion, and how much they benefitted sentient beings through their enlightenment. Contemplate these things and develop strong devotion for all the lineage gurus, such as Milarepa. That will also help you develop devotion to your root guru. When you take a lineage guru such as Jigten Sumgön as your root guru, do supplications, meditate, receive blessings and empowerments, and then dissolve him into yourself so that you become inseparable from him. That is exactly the way to practice guru yoga. Because the great teachers perfected the practice of bodhichitta, their minds pervade all sentient beings. They concern themselves with the suffering of all sentient beings, and they perform activities to benefit all sentient beings. When we take advantage of the opportunity to study and practice, we have the complete opportunity to receive their blessings. It is important that the root guru have all the necessary qualities that the texts describe, not just a title.

A Guru Yoga that Brings the Dharmakaya onto the Path

This concise guru yoga practice, *A Guru Yoga that Brings the Dharmakaya onto the Path*, begins with taking refuge, which is recited three times:

> Vajradhara Guru, embodiment of the Three Jewels,
> I take refuge in you,
> and will until I attain enlightenment.

Taking refuge is the foundation for enlightenment; it is the supreme method to become a buddha. Thus, it is important to engage in its practice with full conviction. Here, we are taking refuge in the dharmakaya, or wisdom mind of the Buddha, which we will eventually actualize and realize ourselves. Buddha Vajradhara is the absolute buddha in dharmakaya form. He is the embodiment of the Buddha, Dharma, and Sangha: Vajradhara's body is the Sangha, Vajradhara's speech is the Dharma, and Vajradhara's mind is Buddha. Until we attain enlightenment, we take refuge in Buddha Vajradhara to eliminate all our obscurations without exception.

Next is the cultivation of bodhichitta, which is also recited three times:

> Sentient beings, victims of the confused projection that is
>   suffering—
> I generate the mindset for enlightenment
> in order to establish you all in the nonabiding state.

Sentient beings means all the beings in samsara who have consciousness or a mind. *Victims of the confused projection that is suffering* means that all sentient beings are victimized by confusion. Because of their confusion, mental afflictions abound in the mind, and nonvirtues and negative karma are created. The result is endless suffering. As long as confusion exists, suffering manifests and arises unceasingly. By considering the helpless sentient beings who are shrouded in delusion and are victims of suffering, we can easily generate great loving-kindness and compassion for them. Bodhichitta, the mind of enlightenment, is developed on that basis. This leads us to vow to end their suffering by establishing them in the *nonabiding state*, the state of buddhahood that doesn't abide in samsara or partial nirvana. We first cultivate these altruistic thoughts and then perfect them with our practice.

After these two preliminary meditations, we turn to the main practice, which we do in order to perfect these two. First, we establish the visualization of Jigten Sumgön:

> Lord Vajradhara Jigten Sumgön sits on a seat of the ten
>   strengths,
> four fearlessnesses, and eighteen unique dharmas;

with major and minor marks of love, compassion,
 and bodhichitta radiating rays of light; and
nonconceptual enlightened activities reaching all migrators equally.

Visualize that Jigten Sumgön spontaneously arises in space in
front of you, sitting on a moon disk, which is atop a sun disk,
which rests on a lotus, which is on a throne supported by
lions. Having achieved ultimate buddhahood, Jigten Sumgön
is inseparable from Buddha Vajradhara; their nature is the
same. That Jigten Sumgön sits on this seat means that he has
attained buddhahood, and so embodies all the perfect qualities of a buddha—the ten strengths, four fearlessnesses, and
eighteen unique dharmas. His physical attributes of major
and minor marks are the product of love, compassion, and
bodhichitta.

Concerning the *ten strengths*, a buddha knows:

1. Places and nonplaces. This means that a buddha
   knows right from wrong, or in other words, knows the
   causality of all things. For example, when you plant
   wheat, you can be sure that wheat will grow and not
   rice. In the same way, virtuous actions result in peace
   and happiness. Nonvirtuous actions result only in
   suffering, never in happiness.

2. Karmic maturation. A buddha knows the exact timing
   of the ripening of karma, what result will come out of
   each action and when.

3. The aspirations of beings, even if the result is hundreds of lifetimes away.

4. The diverse dispositions of beings.

5. The faculties of sentient beings, whether superior or inferior.
6. The destination of every path within samsara and nirvana.
7. The establishment of all stages of meditation, such as the *dhyana* of definite release, samadhi, and *samapatti*.
8. The former abodes that he and all others have resided in from beginningless time.
9. Insight into the future rebirths of beings.
10. The exhaustion of outflows of karmic afflictions.

Concerning the *four fearlessnesses*, a buddha has no fear of:

1. Proclaiming about himself, "All that is to be discarded has been discarded." When Buddha Shakyamuni attained buddhahood, he said that he had purified all obscurations without exception. His statement could not be refuted, so he had no hesitation to proclaim his perfect abandonment of obscurations.
2. Proclaiming about himself, "I possess all qualities." Buddha Shakyamuni said that when he became a buddha, he achieved the two wisdoms: the wisdom of knowing everything as it is and the wisdom of knowing everything in samsara and nirvana. Again, his statement concerning his perfect realization is irrefutable.
3. Proclaiming for others, "This is the path that is the remedy." The Buddha told his followers what path to follow, what meditation to do, and so forth as befitted their disposition. No one could refute that his path leads to liberation.
4. Proclaiming for others, "These are the obscurations to be discarded." The Buddha said that ignorance and mental afflictions are the causes of suffering and must

be discarded. No one can say that these obscurations were not hindrances to enlightenment.

Concerning the *eighteen unique dharmas*, or unshared qualities, it is said that:

1. A buddha is never confused. Even bodhisattvas on the tenth bhumi still have an imprint or tendency of confusion or obscuration, although it is rather subtle. But a buddha has purified all confusion without exception.

2. A buddha is not noisy, which means that he does not engage in idle talk. A buddha speaks when it is necessary and, other than that, he does not waste any time.

3. A buddha never forgets. This means that the Buddha has not forgotten anything, from the limitless eons before his enlightenment, to what happened in that lifetime, up to this moment. Everything is precise, clear, and unmistaken. We may study something today and much of it is forgotten by tomorrow. So many people get dementia and forget things, even the names of their close relatives and friends. The best medicine for that is meditation. You have to practice loving-kindness and compassion to purify, as much as possible, all the mental afflictions. The more you are mindful, relaxed, and calm, the better chance you have of not forgetting. The Buddha is always in a meditative state. Likewise, great masters who have achieved a very high level of meditative equipoise have such a clear mind. This is not just a Buddhist belief, this is a method that will work for everyone. Buddha did not teach the solution to suffering as a belief, but as a method we can practice.

The remaining unshared qualities are self-explanatory.

4. A buddha never loses meditative equipoise.
5. A buddha does not have any perception of discursiveness.
6. A buddha's equanimity is not due to a lack of discernment.
7. A buddha's motivation never degenerates.
8. A buddha's perseverance never degenerates.
9. A buddha's mindfulness never degenerates.
10. A buddha's meditative concentration never degenerates.
11. A buddha's wisdom never degenerates.
12. A buddha's complete liberation never degenerates.
13. A buddha's every action of the body is preceded by wisdom and followed by wisdom.
14. A buddha's every action of speech is preceded by wisdom and followed by wisdom.
15. A buddha's every action of mind is preceded by wisdom and followed by wisdom.
16. A buddha sees the past through wisdom that is unattached and unobstructed.
17. A buddha sees the future through wisdom that is unattached and unobstructed.
18. A buddha sees the present through wisdom that is unattached and unobstructed.

Knowing these ten strengths, four fearlessnesses, and eighteen unshared qualities helps us gain greater clarity about the nature shared by all buddhas, including Buddha Vajradhara, Buddha Shakyamuni, and Jigten Sumgön.

In this visualization, we see Jigten Sumgön's perfect form as being insubstantial, like a rainbow, its appearance and emptiness inseparable. Light radiates out in all directions, taking his enlightened activities to every sentient being equally until the end of samsara.

The next part of this guru yoga practice is the mantra recitation. Repeat this mantra as many times as you can while maintaining the visualization:

OM AH RATNA SHRI SARVA SIDDHI HUM

Om, ah, and *hum* indicate the body, speech, and mind of a buddha. *Ratna shri* is another name for Jigten Sumgön. *Sarva siddhi* means "all attainment or achievement," which includes mahamudra, the highest realization. So the meaning of the mantra is, "May I and every sentient being achieve a buddha's qualities, including mahamudra."

During the recitation of the mantra, meditate that the light of love and compassion manifests from Jigten Sumgön's entire body, especially from his forehead, throat, and heart. This light pervades every sentient being in the six realms, purifying all of their obscurations, suffering, and causes of suffering. This exercises your own love, compassion, and bodhichitta. See that all sentient beings are inhaling the light as peace and joy, and rejoice in this.

Then comes the blessing supplication:

You are the buddhas Nagakulapradipa and Dipankara of the past,
Maitreya of the future, and Shakyamuni of the present;
the reincarnation of Nagarjuna; the peerless Ratna Shri—
Lord Jigten Sumgön, I supplicate you.

Blessing supplication means to receive blessings by invoking the qualities of an enlightened being, in this case, the qualities of Jigten Sumgön. Countless eons ago, the peerless Ratna Shri, Jigten Sumgön, perfected all the activities of a buddha. He attained enlightenment in the distant past and was known as Buddha Nagakulapradipa, and again later as Buddha Dipankara. In the future, Maitreya will be a great reincarnation of Jigten Sumgön. In our present age, Jigten Sumgön is an embodiment of Buddha Shakyamuni. He is also the reincarnation of Nagarjuna, who was responsible for revitalizing the Buddha's teachings, especially the Mahayana and Vajrayana teachings.

As the embodiment of all the buddhas of the past, present, and future, we can confidently take Jigten Sumgön as a root guru and totally rely on his wisdom and compassion. Supplicate from the bottom of your heart for him to bless you, to help you to purify your obscurations and negative karma so that you can practice bodhichitta successfully and benefit sentient beings.

In response to your supplication, the guru bestows empowerment:

> Light rays emanate from the guru's body, speech, and
>   mind
> and dissolve into my four places,
> thereby purifying the four obscurations, bestowing
>   the four empowerments,
> and planting the seeds of the four kayas.
> The guru then dissolves into me.
> My mind is natural luminosity-emptiness.

After praying and reciting the mantra, we receive the four empowerments. This is called "receiving empowerment through meditation," and is an especially powerful method for transformation. As you reinforce the enlightened qualities within yourself, you have an opportunity to completely purify all your obscurations and receive the blessing of all the buddhas. The method to receive the four empowerments and how to meditate on them follows. When you receive these empowerments as described with full meditative attention, step by step purification can be accomplished.

From Jigten Sumgön's forehead, white lights radiate. They have the nature of the wisdom body of all the buddhas. They dissolve into your forehead and pervade your entire body. Meditate that all the obscurations and negative karma of the body are purified, and that your body's appearance and emptiness are inseparable. Through this you receive the vase empowerment, which plants the seed to achieve *nirmanakaya*, the emanation body of a buddha.

Then, from Jigten Sumgön's throat, red lights manifest. They have the nature of all the buddhas' wisdom speech. They dissolve into your throat and pervade your entire body. Meditate that all the negative karma and obscurations related to speech are fully purified, and that your speech's sound and emptiness are inseparable. Through this you receive the secret empowerment, which plants the seed to achieve *sambhogakaya*, the enjoyment body of a buddha.

Then, from Jigten Sumgön's heart, blue lights manifest. They have the nature of all the buddhas' wisdom. They dissolve into your heart and pervade your entire body. Meditate that all mental obscurations and afflictions are fully purified and that your mind's clarity and emptiness are inseparable.

Through this you receive the wisdom empowerment, and by thus meditating that your mind is the nature of space, the seed to achieve dharmakaya, the wisdom body of a buddha, is planted.

Then, from Jigten Sumgön's navel, golden lights manifest. The golden lights represent all the qualities of the buddhas. They dissolve into your navel and pervade your entire body. Meditate that all the subtle obscurations of body, speech, and mind are fully purified. Through this you receive the fourth empowerment, through which you receive all the qualities of the buddhas and the seed to achieve the *svabhavikakaya*, the nature body of a buddha, is planted.

At the end, Jigten Sumgön dissolves into light. That light enters the crown of your head and flows down to pervade your entire body. Then your body dissolves into emptiness. You should continue to meditate by perceiving that your mind has the nature of space. Do not chase the past or future; just let it be as it is, in emptiness and luminosity. All afflictions and mental delusions have dissolved into luminous emptiness. The mind is clear, precise, tranquil, serene, and peaceful. This is the method to unite your mind with the buddha-mind that is free of all boundaries and limitations. Just rest there. Meditate there as long as you like.

When your meditation is complete, dedicate the accumulated virtue:

> Through both the innate virtue
> and the virtue accumulated in the three times by all in
>   samsara and nirvana,
> may I and all sentient beings filling space, none left out,

realize the coemergent ultimate reality and
attain the final state of nonabidance in existence or peace.

We gather the accumulation of virtues within the mandala of
bodhichitta and dedicate the entire collection to the enlightenment of every sentient being, without leaving even one
behind. The *three times* are the past, present, and future. *All in
samsara* refers to sentient beings in the six realms of samsara,
which include animals, hell beings, hungry ghosts, humans,
demigods, and gods; *all in nirvana* refers to buddhas, bodhisattvas, pratyekabuddhas, and shravakas in nirvana. We dedicate the virtue of our practice so that all beings may actualize
mahamudra, the nature of their own mind without fabrication, like the nature of space. By realizing that, we attain the
final state of *nonabidance in existence or peace*, which means one
abides neither in samsara nor in partial nirvana.

As you can see, this practice is concise and easy to do, yet
profound. You can practice at any time, morning or evening.
Once you're more accustomed to it, you won't even need to
use the text. It will be very useful as you approach the time of
your death because you will be able to remain calm and will
be well-prepared for the early stages of the dying process.
Whether you have the energy to say it aloud or not, simply
visualize Jigten Sumgön, take refuge mentally, cultivate bodhichitta for the benefit of sentient beings, chant the mantra quietly, develop devotion, receive the four empowerments, let
the guru dissolve into you, and receive all the blessings. Maintain your mind like space with a feeling of gratitude. Rejoice
in your own good fortune and yearn for all sentient beings to

have the same. Dedicate the virtue of your practice without attachment to this and that, here and there. Your rebirth will be much better for this.

Devadatta, seeing His greatness,
became envious
and, losing control over his meditation,
did many improper things.

With his mind sullied,
he created a schism in the Sage's community,
and by reason of the separation, instead of being devoted to Him,
he endeavored to do Him harm.

Then he set a rock rolling with force on Mount Gridhrakuta;
but though aimed at the Sage,
it did not fall on Him but divided into two pieces.

On the royal highway,
he set loose in the direction of the Tathagata a lord of elephants,
whose trumpeting was as the thundering of the black clouds at the
    dissolution of the world,
and whose rushing was as the wind in the sky when the moon
    is obscured.

The streets of Rajagriha became impassable through the corpses,
which he had struck with his body or taken up with his trunk
or whose entrails were drawn out by his tusks and scattered in
    heaps. [. . .]

Despite the oncoming elephant intent on slaughter,
despite the weeping people holding up their arms [in warning],
the Blessed One advanced, collected and unmoved,
not breaking His step nor giving way to malevolence. [. . .]

Then, as the enraged elephant drew near,
he came to his senses through the Sage's spiritual power,
and, letting his body down,
he placed his head on the ground like a mountain shattered by
    a thunderbolt.
—Ashvagosha, *Buddhacarita*

CHAPTER 4

Vulture Peak: The *Heart Sutra*

Ancient Rajagriha, known today as Rajgir, holds a significant place in the Buddha's history, and is honored as one of the eight great Buddhist pilgrimage sites. The Buddha visited here many times, both before and after his enlightenment. It was the capital of Magadha, the seat of the Buddha's greatest patron, King Bimbisara. The town was nestled within five steep, rocky hills and surrounded by a protective stone wall. Some of the twenty-five miles of the wall still stand twelve feet high and seventeen feet thick.

A year after his enlightenment, the Buddha made his first return to Rajagriha and arrived with a thousand monks. King Bimbisara was inspired to offer Venuvana, the Bamboo Grove, for the site of the first Buddhist monastery. The grove was perfectly situated for meditation, given it was not too near the city, had a pleasant climate, and had access to fresh water. The Buddha spent at least five rains retreats there. Today, little remains of the monastery but a large garden inside a fenced park. In the center of the park is a bathing pool that was used by the Buddha.

In later years, the Buddha's cousin Devadatta plotted in

many ways to take over leadership of the sangha. Hoping that the loss of his patron, King Bimbisara, would lead to the Buddha's downfall, Devadatta convinced the king's son, Ajatashatru, to imprison his father and starve him to death. The remains of the prison's foundation can be seen today. Devadatta also once tried to harm the Buddha by hurling a large rock at him while he was walking in the vicinity of Vulture Peak. The rock split into two pieces, and is still there. The blow caused injury to the Buddha's foot. He was treated by the physician Jivaka, who later donated a mango plantation to the Buddha as a resting place at the base of the road that leads to Vulture Peak. Ruins of three large halls are all that remain of the Jivaka Amravana Vihara built there.

Finally, Devadatta attempted to kill the Buddha by setting Nalagiri, a notoriously ferocious elephant, on him while he was begging in Rajagriha. This, too, was thwarted when the Buddha calmed the rushing elephant with a few words of loving-kindness. A large brick stupa that is traditionally said to commemorate this event stands near a wall surrounding the older part of Rajagriha.

To the east of Rajagriha, just outside its ring of five protective peaks, is Gridhrakuta, Vulture Peak. It was so named because of a rock formation that resembles a sitting vulture and for the birds that once lived in the area. King Bimbisara built a royal road up to the peak to facilitate hearing the Buddha teach. Here, there is no question that one is walking exactly the same road that the Buddha did; the rocks alongside the trail are the same ones that he passed by. Further up the road are two stupas that mark King Bimbisara's journey up to see the Buddha. Two natural caves toward the top are known to have been used to shelter the Buddha and his disciples.

Atop the peak is a paved terrace and the low walls of a small shrine encircling a statue of the meditating Buddha. On this sacred site, the Buddha delivered some of his most significant teachings, those of the Prajnaparamita (Perfection of Wisdom), to countless human and nonhuman listeners.

The bodhisattva Chandraprabha Kumara (Youthful Moonlight) requested the *Samadhiraja Sutra*, the sutra form of the mahamudra teachings, in the Rajagriha area. Thousands gathered and the Buddha taught for many days. At the end, the Buddha prophesied that Chandraprabha Kumara would be reborn as Gampopa.

One significant event happened in this area shortly after the Buddha's *parinirvana*: five hundred of the most senior monks assembled in order to compile a complete collection of the Buddha's teachings. This First Buddhist Council took place at the Sattapani caves on Vaibhara Hill between old and new Rajagriha. The land was offered by then-king Ajatashatru, who had renounced his former evil deeds and become a devout patron like his father.

The land around what is known today as Rajgir was not always a holy place, but rather it became holy by the presence of the Buddha and, in particular, by the precious teachings he gave here. The Buddha turned the wheel of Dharma three times. The first turning was at Sarnath, where he taught the four noble truths. The second turning was at Vulture Peak, and the third was at Vaishali and Kushinagar. At Vulture Peak, the Buddha taught all of the Prajnaparamita, the Perfection of Wisdom teachings, and many other Mahayana sutras. The Prajnaparamita literature includes the *Heart Sutra*, the *Diamond Sutra*, and several sutras named for the number of lines they contain, such as the *8,000-Line Prajnaparamita*,

25,000-Line *Prajnaparamita*, 100,000-Line *Prajnaparamita*, and so forth. The wisdom that is to be perfected is not mere worldly knowledge. Rather, in Buddhism, wisdom refers to the mind of critical insight that penetrates into the nature of reality, the pure nature of the mind. The pure nature of the mind is the buddha nature that every sentient being possesses. That nature is not defiled by any obscurations or delusions.

Even though the essence of mind is pure, adventitious delusion leads to all different types of suffering. Our confusion creates the causes of suffering. Even though we want to be free from suffering, throughout our life we engage in activities such as politics, business, science, and technology; our entire life is dedicated to keeping busy. We think we are seeking peace and happiness, but without the wisdom of critical insight and being ignorant of virtue and nonvirtue, suffering comes endlessly no matter what we do. This is why the teaching about how to cut through delusion is critically important. Actually, everyone needs this wisdom. It is not something just to believe in; it is a method, a means to become completely free from suffering.

Lifestyles may have changed since the time of the Buddha and philosophies may have developed, but the wisdom of causality has never changed. The cause of our suffering now is the same cause of suffering that the Buddha first taught. Likewise, the cause of peace and happiness is still the same cause of peace and happiness that the Buddha taught. Similarly, fire was hot and air was light at the time of the Buddha, and that has never changed. That is why this wisdom is called the nature of the reality of *all* phenomena. If we apply it in our meditation practice, it will purify our mental obscurations— ignorance, attachment, aversion, greed, and so forth. These mental afflictions are the real causes of suffering, whether someone knows it or not, or whether they believe it or not. The perfection of wisdom is the indispensable method to cut suffering off at the root.

Since everything exists subject to the law of causality, results are inevitable, because they depend entirely on their associated causes. That is interdependence. Our understanding of the function of interdependence, that very nature, is what we call emptiness. Thus, we can say that interdependence and emptiness are inseparable. This is not just a Buddhist belief, but how reality actually functions. Whoever makes the effort to capture this wisdom really does have a chance to become free from suffering.

The *Heart Sutra*

In the opening lines of the *Heart Sutra*, we see that it was at Vulture Peak that a great assembly of monks and bodhisattvas came together. At that time, the Buddha was in the meditative state of equipoise called "appearance of the profound."[3] Here, "profound" refers to emptiness. Why is it called profound? This emptiness is not like a cup being empty of water. Rather, emptiness is a state where our conceptual thoughts and dualistic mind cannot penetrate. It can only be captured by the synchronicity of meditative equipoise and critical insight. Without judgment or imposition, one directly sees the wisdom of emptiness. This wisdom of emptiness allows unafflicted compassion and all the rest of the Buddha's excellent qualities to manifest.

The nature of all composite phenomena can be understood by examining the five *skandhas*, or aggregates:

1. *Form* refers to the colors and shapes that we see, the sense organs (eyes, ears, nose, tongue, and body), and the sensory objects (sights, sounds, smells, tastes, and tactile objects).
2. *Feelings* are of three types: suffering, joy, and neutrality.
3. *Perception* involves perceiving an object as good, bad, or neutral.
4. *Mental formation* is creating karma through mental faculties.
5. *Consciousness* consists of the eye consciousness, ear consciousness, tongue consciousness, body consciousness, nose consciousness, and mental consciousness.

Thus, while the Buddha was abiding in that meditation, the bodhisattva Avalokiteshvara contemplated the nature of emptiness of the five aggregates. The five aggregates are the basis of all composite phenomena, all of samsara and nirvana, including the four elements: earth, water, air, and fire. Even the precious human life depends on these five. They are naturally impermanent, the basis of our suffering, of the karma we create, and the results we experience. Having understood the reality nature of the five aggregates within samsara, we are moved to take refuge in the Buddha, Dharma, and Sangha to be free from the vicious cycle of suffering. Then we cultivate bodhichitta in order to develop further mental qualities. Through these processes, these very five aggregates gradually transform into a foundation for enlightenment. For example, if we visualize our body in an enlightened deity's form, the aggregates transform into the enlightened state. If we practice mahamudra within the context of wisdom and compassion, that itself is the enlightened state. This is how to ground our practice. Thus, it is very important to have a clear understanding of these five skandhas as the basis of suffering and, when we are awakened from delusion, as the basis for enlightenment.

By the inspiration and blessings of the Buddha, Shariputra asked Avalokiteshvara how someone of noble family, who is interested in this meditation practice on the emptiness of the five aggregates, should train in the practice. Avalokiteshvara's reply makes up the bulk of the *Heart Sutra*. It starts, "Shariputra, any noble son or noble daughter who so wishes to engage in the practice of the profound perfection of wisdom should clearly see this way . . ." and continues in detail. What is perhaps the most famous summary of wisdom is recorded in this sutra:

> Form is emptiness, emptiness is form; emptiness is not other than form, form too is not other than emptiness. Likewise, feelings, perceptions, mental formations, and consciousness are all empty.

This is a very succinct restatement of a profound and complex concept. Saying that form is emptiness means that emptiness is the nature of all phenomena. In other words, everything manifests out of emptiness; no phenomenon exists inherently under its own power. On the other hand, saying that emptiness is form points to the fact that there is no need to look for emptiness anywhere else—it is form. There is no separation between them, no duality.

The Eight Aspects of Emptiness

The *Heart Sutra* mentions eight aspects of emptiness by saying, "Therefore, Shariputra, all phenomena are emptiness; they are without defining characteristics; they are not born, they do not cease; they are not defiled, they are not undefiled; they are not deficient, and they are not complete." Let's explore these eight aspects of emptiness more in depth.

1. All phenomena are emptiness.

Saying that the nature of all phenomena, which are composed of the five aggregates, is emptiness means that they cannot exist or function without external support. They are merely manifestations that appear through the interaction of many causes and conditions. This kind of emptiness is ultimate wisdom, not conventional knowledge, such as a cup being empty of tea. This emptiness is the profound realization of the nonexistent nature of reality as we know it. Emptiness is not an obscure Buddhist philosophy pursued by a few academics. It is the true nature of all phenomena without exception.

For example, examine mental afflictions. Everyone in the world is under the control of the mental afflictions of attachment, aversion, and ignorance. No matter how smart we are, no matter how creative we are with technology, we are still not smart enough to see the nature of the flow of our unceasing thoughts. We never think about how to purify this mental outflow; we only feed it. Without such an investigation into the nature of these thoughts, they are real and powerful. Without the wisdom of insight, we remain completely under their domination. No matter how much effort we make to escape this vicious cycle, the suffering continues.

On the other hand, if we were to examine our thoughts, we would see that they are evanescent, ephemeral, as fleeting as a cloud. We could study the suffering we endure; we could apply critical insight and see how mental afflictions enslave us. The way we blindly repeat the same actions and the way we are profoundly habituated in affliction would become obvious. Slowly we can realize that instead of being real and powerful, our habitual thoughts are merely the adventitious result of causes and conditions.

Based on this inkling of wisdom, we can start to develop a sense of renunciation toward suffering. This leads us to look at the cause of our mental and physical suffering and search for a way to counteract it. We start doing the practices that, step by step, dismantle the habits that cause our suffering. Then it becomes possible to develop the wisdom that directly perceives everything as illusory, as clear appearance without essence. This is the true nature of our mind, whether we understand it or not.

The purpose of studying, and especially of practicing, emptiness is that it is the direct method to eliminate suffering and defeat the causes of suffering. The more we see the empty nature of phenomena, the more effective our practice becomes. We will deeply see that there is no benefit to being attached to illusory manifestations, that there is nothing to feel aversion toward. But just learning about emptiness is not enough. We must also focus on applying it in practice—not through religious belief, but based on our empirical experience. In this way, we can finally come to the point of experiencing everything within the context of emptiness. No one can hand this understanding to you. Each individual must traverse their own journey to the cessation of suffering.

2. Phenomena are without defining characteristics.

Since all external and internal phenomena are of the nature of emptiness, they have no defining characteristics. There are two ways to understand this: through philosophical reasoning and through practical experience. As you investigate the five aggregates of feeling, perception, and the rest, look at each one and ask yourself, "Where is the body?" From the head to the legs, you will find no independent form. If there is no inherently existent body, what is it that has feeling, perception, mental formation, or consciousness?

Once we are convinced through analysis about how phenomena truly function, we can apply this wisdom to our practice. First look at how everything is impermanent, changing every second. It is a small step from there to the realization that phenomena are illusory, like a reflection of the moon in a lake. Nothing real exists, just reflections and manifestations. But unless you practice this, meaning that you habituate yourself in this wisdom, there is no practical benefit to mere information. Through practice, the grip of fixation gradually releases and is replaced by the experience of peace and harmony. When you actually experience the body as emptiness, nothing remains to be categorized as suffering or pain. This is called realization.

3. Phenomena are not born.

Of course, from the conventional point of view there is birth. Seeds germinate and mothers give birth to children. We are not ignoring these facts when we say phenomena are not born. Rather, we are looking at our world from a different perspective, that of emptiness and the wisdom that all phenomena are illusory. We are purifying our mental grasping that treats birth as real by understanding that nothing exists in that way. Because phenomena don't exist, they could not have been born; we cannot identify a starting point.

Thoughts arise unceasingly; they manifest from emptiness and dissolve back into emptiness. Just let them be. Don't fixate on them. Don't dwell on thoughts as good or bad. That is known as wisdom. Once you experience your thoughts this way, you are touching close to the true nature of reality, which is free of fabrications. Let go and remain in that uncontrived nature; here there is no fear because there is no attachment. Relax where you are and be aware of the thought process as it manifests and fades due to the arising of causes and conditions. Thoughts come one after another like clouds in the sky. If you try to pin them down, they disappear; their nature is empty. Release the fixations that trap you as if encased in a cocoon. This is the benefit of reflecting on the unborn nature of phenomena. At the same time that you are developing this wisdom, it is important to cultivate great compassion for all the sentient beings who are also trapped in this hellish state with no hope of release.

4. Phenomena do not cease.

Because nothing begins, there are no phenomena to abide or cease. On the relative level, we know that those who are born will die, that whatever comes into existence will cease to exist. However, from the ultimate point of view, both birth and cessation are illusory. There is nothing substantial to grasp. The practitioners and highly accomplished masters abide without suffering within the nature of the unborn and unceasing.

5. Phenomena are not defiled.
No defilements exist within emptiness, within reality as it is. The nature of mind itself is ease and peace, right from the beginning. Since that is the case, there is nothing to be labeled "impure" or "afflicted." There is no defilement because defilement itself is empty, so it is not enough to just say "free of defilement." We must develop the critical insight to see that for ourselves.

6. Phenomena are not undefiled.
Phenomena themselves do not exist, so there is nothing to purify, and nothing from which to separate defilements. In addition, purity is a concept that does not have a place within nonconceptual emptiness.

7. Phenomena are not deficient.
The buddha nature at the core of every sentient being is innately pure, and has been since beginningless time. There has never been any separation between ourselves and the excellent qualities and wisdom of a buddha. Thus, nothing needs to be added in order to experience our own buddhahood, to see our own enlightened nature.

8. Phenomena are not complete.
All the thoughts that appear to our mind are fabrications; the nature of these thoughts is emptiness. The mental afflictions that obscure the wisdom that sees things as they truly are exist nowhere. Thus, as we progress toward enlightenment, there is nothing to subtract from our mind as nothing was there in the first place. This realization of mind as it is is unfabricated, uncontrived wisdom.

Understanding Emptiness

Samsara and nirvana are concepts that abide within the sphere of emptiness. Samsara is the state of liberation distorted by the lens of dualistic thought based in ignorance. When we reflect on this and finally realize that the confusion of samsara is empty, that itself is nirvana. Samsara is not different from nirvana, but unless we personally realize this truth, "real" suffering will remain. It is ironic that we use so many words to express the inexpressible nature of emptiness. We do this to facilitate the transition from the relative to the ultimate points of view. Again, our habitual view of reality is so entrenched that we need all this analysis and explanation to make sure we get the message.

The problem is that our innate wisdom is obscured by ignorance. We are completely habituated in duality, a habit so effortless that we are generally unaware of it. When the mind is obscured by grasping at duality, the negative mental factors of attachment, aversion, and so forth arise without effort. Even though their nature is illusory and empty, we are so deeply habituated and so entangled in confusion that we have no chance to get rid of them. The afflictions, in turn, create the causes of suffering. It is not enough just to say that we do not want to suffer; we must look into our mind and purify these delusions. All phenomena exist relatively—that is, they depend on the coming together of many causes and conditions. Everything is interdependent, and the very nature of this interconnectedness is emptiness. We need unwavering conviction and courage to follow this path.

Emptiness is more than a simplistic idea of nothingness or a void. We must go beyond that belief and directly perceive that phenomena, including the five aggregates, do not exist as we usually perceive them, and understand that they ultimately exist within the framework of emptiness. However, we all communicate and function within relative truth. All causalities operate within relative truth. Everything, every being and phenomenon, has a distinct cause and condition. Results infallibly arise from their corresponding causes; thus it is called inexorable karmic causation.

Karma is not a cultural belief. In Sanskrit, *karma* means "action." Whatever action stems from one's body, speech, or mind becomes the cause for an effect that will be experienced later. The nature of this relative state is emptiness, as earlier mentioned. Nothing and no one exists independently without the support of others; that very emptiness encompasses all the manifestations of the relative state. This process is called dependent arising. Those who are enlightened experience this precisely without any separation between emptiness and relative manifestations. From their point of view, all delusions have been transcended; delusion has no space to function. There is nothing to grasp, nothing to hate, nothing to fixate on. In contrast, our dualistic mind has little wisdom and remains entangled within the relative state due to ignorance. Grasping, anger, aversion, attachment, and all our suffering follow from this. Even though we don't want suffering, we have no choice once we create its cause. Therefore, we must take care of the causes we are creating instead of just wishing for a positive result.

Understanding is the first step toward wisdom. Then contemplation and practice are very important to habituate this understanding in your mind. We can study, contemplate and then practice these topics: eighteen *dhatus*, twelve *ayatanas*, five skandhas, twelve links of interdependence and their reverse, and the four noble truths and their reverse (see glossary of enumerations). With that kind of support, we gradually purify mental delusion, ignorance, and afflicting emotions. Analysis, investigation, and debate can theoretically prove that nothing exists independently, but if we don't put our theory into practice and use it to purify our obscurations, we won't gain much benefit. Here, practice means seeing everything as a manifestation with an illusory nature, a mere reflection of karma and mind. The entire purpose of our study, contemplation, and practice is to free ourselves from suffering and to experience peace and happiness in our daily life, and ultimately achieve absolute buddhahood. All that we know in samsara is like a mirage, like the moon's reflection in a lake, like a rainbow, or like a dream. Phenomena exist and function only with the support of many causes and conditions. Thus, we know that they are not inherently real. With the help of these examples, we can start to understand that everything in samsara is illusory in nature, including our suffering and happiness. Personally experiencing this will release us from the grasping and fixated mind and allow the mind of freedom to shine forth.

There are two concepts regarding the self that we are to purify: the concept of a personal self and of the self of phenomena. Through countless lifetimes, we have become habituated in the propensity to regard these two as real. This is so deeply rooted that when we meditate on the selflessness of persons or phenomena, we feel it is artificial and contrived. We need a productive and powerful remedy to heal our wounded mind, so we meditate on everything being an illusion and empty in order to deconstruct this habit. But it is not enough just to learn about emptiness; we also need to emphasize compassion. We require powerful motivation and a recognition that the Buddha gave us a great method to free ourselves from bondage.

Because of ignorance, we hold on to or grasp the personal self. On the basis of this personal self, thoughts of "I" and "my" arise and attachment manifests. Once there is an "I" and attachment to oneself, then the idea of "other" comes quickly and aversion manifests. These two, self and other, become the foundation for attachment and aversion. From these, we create various and countless karmas, which in turn create the whole of the six realms. The root source for all of this is ignorance. Emptiness is the only method to release this endless cycle. If you want to be freed from the suffering of samsara, there is no alternative to the wisdom of emptiness. That is why it is so important to study and practice the *Heart Sutra*.

A Concise Explanation of the Mantra

The famous mantra of the *Heart Sutra* is TADYATHA GATÉ GATÉ PARAGATÉ PARASAMGATÉ BODHI SVAHA. The translation is "Gone, gone, gone beyond, gone perfectly beyond, and established in enlightenment, buddhahood." *Gaté*, pronounced *gah tay*, can also be translated as "realized."

The first gaté means we are aware that we are in samsara and that we have realized that its nature is suffering. Suffering here does not refer only to literal pain, but also to pervasive, or conditioned, suffering. Even if we should experience some peace, joy, or happiness in the desire, form, and formless realms of samsara, it is only temporary. Within samsara, impermanence and suffering circle one after the other. When you see that reality directly and genuinely renounce samsara, you take the first step toward enlightenment. Then one starts accumulating merit and wisdom and engages in the practice of calm abiding, or *shamatha*. This realization is called accomplishment of the path of accumulation, and it consists of the four mindfulnesses, four abandonments, and four foundations of miracle powers.

The second *gaté* means that you progress further and meditate with the support of the five powers and five strengths. You establish the state of meditative equipoise by relaxing your mind. Within that state of equipoise, all mental activity is calmed. When you achieve the meditative state of total equipoise, there is a great opportunity to see things clearly and perceive the deeper meaning of suffering directly. You are more inspired to free yourself from samsara. This is called the path of application.

Paragaté means to go beyond samsara by uprooting the delusion of ignorance with the support of the seven branches of enlightenment. On the path of insight, you continue to meditate in order to remove the latent conceptions of inherent existence and to perceive all-pervading emptiness directly. You realize the nonexistent nature of ignorance, and selflessness is understood.

Parasamgaté means to go perfectly beyond. When you have realized this state, you stabilize your meditation to purify the psychic imprints of the habitual tendencies of samsara and subtle conceptions of the self of person and phenomena. You progress to the path of meditation supported by the noble eightfold path. We continue this way, progressing step by step through the second to tenth bhumis, until we have gone perfectly beyond samsara.

Bodhi svaha means enlightenment is accomplished. After purifying all the gross and subtle obscurations, without anything remaining, there is bodhi, complete enlightenment.

As you chant this mantra, meditate on its meaning. This is just a brief introduction to the meaning of the terms. The mantra actually has vast and profound meaning that could not be fully described in many lifetimes.

There are two levels of interpretation of this mantra: the physical and mental. Physically, we are aging. We are born as a baby, then go through childhood, adulthood, old age, and finally we die. So on the level of interpretation in physical terms, the mantra means that we go endlessly from life to life in this way. When we go through these stages we should recall the impermanence of life and the vicious cycle of samsara. At the end of the day, the only benefit we receive comes from our practice of these precious teachings. With this, we can die peacefully and joyfully without fear or confusion and eventually achieve enlightenment.

Regarding the interpretation of the mantra on the mental level, it is important to meditate to release all obscurations from your mind. Without the Buddha's teachings, the mental obscurations will not disappear by themselves as we get older. The Buddha's teaching is indispensable, so apply the Perfection of Wisdom teaching to the mind and release your confusion and delusion step by step, as explained above. We need mindfulness, interest, and devotion so that we can eventually become free from samsara and attain buddhahood.

Now take a moment to relax physically and mentally. Take a deep breath and exhale all your tension. Release attachments and fixations. Look at all the sentient beings in the world:

those who are educated and uneducated, those who are rich and poor, those who are young and old. Every one of them is under the control of mental affliction and karma, and in a state of suffering. Cultivate a sense of strong compassion, yearning for them all to be free from their suffering. Then meditate that the very nature of suffering and its causes is emptiness. They exist nowhere. But in ignorance, the dualistic mind wanders between hope and fear. Understand the true nature of mind and meditate without hope or fear in the full meaning of emptiness.

If you have time, chant the *Heart Sutra* (written in full in appendix B) in a contemplative way. At the end, dedicate your practice to the enlightenment of everyone in the world.

Udbhata and his brother provided five hundred sravaka monks with livelihood in Vajrasana and entertained five hundred followers of the Mahayana at Nalanda. Nalanda, the birth-place of Shariputra, was also the place where Shariputra, along with eighty thousand arhats, later attained nirvana. In the meanwhile, the brahmana settlement there fell into ruins. Only the caitya of Shariputra remained. King Asoka elaborately worshiped it and built a large temple of the Buddha there. The first five hundred acaryas of the Mahayana discussed among themselves and came to know that if the Mahayana was preached at the place of Shariputra, it was going to be extensively spread. However, if it was preached at the place of Maudgalyayana, [the Buddhists] were going to be very powerful without greatly spreading the Doctrine. So the two acaryas—the brahmarta brothers—built eight temples [at Nalanda] and placed there all the scriptures of the Mahayana. Thus Asoka was the founder of the first vihara at Nalanda. The five hundred acaryas along with Udbhata and his brother enlarged the centre. Rahulabhadra spread the Doctrine [of Mahayana] still further and Nagarjuna made it most extensive.
—Taranatha, *The History of Buddhism in India*

CHAPTER 5

Nalanda: Shantideva and the Bodhisattva's Way of Life

VERY LITTLE REMAINS of the once-magnificent university at Nalanda, but what survives is quite impressive. Excavations to date have revealed two-story-high walls of eleven monasteries and six large temples. Based on credible accounts of there having been upwards of 10,000 residents at its height, only a small portion of the original buildings have been located and unearthed. Identical living quarters stretch out in a long line; each would have housed between sixty and eighty monks. There is also evidence of an extensive drainage system, paved walkways, and wells. Rising above the campus is Shariputra's stupa, which was originally constructed by King Ashoka and repeatedly enlarged by later royal dynasties. The surrounding area is filled with many small stupas. In addition to the archaeological site, a nearby museum displays fine examples of the famous religious sculptures once produced at Nalanda, as well as coins, pottery, and other artifacts uncovered by the excavations.

While the official founding of the famous university is dated in the second or third century CE, the site was well known before that because it was on the main trade route between Rajagriha and the Ganges River. Centuries before it was established as the world's first university, the Buddha stopped at Nalanda and taught many times. The Buddha met the great Mahakashyapa there; his foremost disciples, Shariputra and Maudgalyayana, were both born nearby; and Shariputra is said to have died there. In the third century BCE, King Ashoka is recorded as having made a pilgrimage to Nalanda and raised a stupa there to house relics of Shariputra.

Nalanda University was founded as a center for the propagation of the Mahayana doctrine. From roughly 400 to 1100 CE, it enjoyed royal patronage under the Gupta and Pala dynasties. Other Buddhist universities, such as Vikramashila, Somapura, Odantapuri, and Jagaddala, were operating around the same time. During that time, Nalanda became an international center for education and the arts with thousands of resident students and teachers. They came from India and many other places, including China, Korea, Tibet, Japan, Indonesia, and Vietnam. Among the distinguished figures associated with Nalanda are Nagarjuna, Asanga, Naropa, Atisha, Dharmakirti, Shantideva, and most of the eighty-four mahasiddhas of India. Of particular significance was its renowned library, said to have been nine stories tall and filled with tens of thousands of texts. When it was destroyed by invaders in the late 1100s, these texts provided enough fuel to burn continuously for months. A precious handful of manuscripts from Nalanda survived and are housed in museums throughout the world. Because of its widespread influence throughout the Buddhist world well beyond India, Nalanda University holds a very important place in history.

Scholarship at Nalanda

Students in this university did more than just worship and say prayers. They carefully studied what the Buddha taught, the three *pitakas* as well as the Vajrayana texts and practices. In the *Gandhavyuha Sutra*, the Buddha said, "You should study what I teach and you should practice what I teach. It is not enough just to worship me or believe in me, but for your own benefit and for the benefit of all other sentient beings, you have to study and practice." The Buddha also taught how to approach his teachings this way:

> O bhikṣus and wise men,
> just as a goldsmith would test his gold
> by burning, cutting, and rubbing it,
> so you must examine my words and accept them.
> But not merely out of reverence for me.[4]

When the Buddha advised us to thoroughly investigate his teachings, he didn't mean for us to look for mistakes. A buddha can never make a mistake because he is fully enlightened. He said we should investigate the profundity and vastness of the teachings, especially the five paths and ten bhumis, so that we would benefit from deep study and better understanding.

In ancient times, people came to Nalanda with reverence and dedication because they saw the great benefit in study and practice. Their education, wisdom, and skills allowed Buddhism to spread freely to many countries. Seeing how successful the ancient practitioners were, we should follow in their footsteps and develop a good understanding of what the Buddha taught and why he taught it, and, of vital importance, put the Dharma into practice. Study and practice must go side by side, for the Buddha's teachings provide a unique opportunity to see the infinite mind.

There are two truths: the relative and the absolute. First we study, scrutinize the teachings, raise questions, and discuss the relative truth. Once we have attained some understanding, we bring the teachings into the mind, into the heart, and apply and practice them in order to actualize the absolute truth, to experience the benefit for ourselves. Using these two methods together, we can purify our mental obscurations one by one. The more we purify our mind, the more negative thoughts, ignorance, and delusion will diminish. Slowly we will see the infinite nature of the mind. Mind is like space; there is no limit to its vastness, no edge, no boundary. Just as space is limitless, our mind is limitless. The only way to capture the limitless nature of the mind is to contemplate its inexpressible nature and practice the sublime Dharma.

Every country in the world emphasizes education because it gives people a chance for a better life. The same is true for the Buddhadharma. Buddhism is an educational religion in the sense that you study and practice in order to gain more understanding, knowledge, and wisdom. Then we develop devotion to the Buddha and to his precious teachings, and bring them into our heart to practice them.

Thus, Buddhism goes a little farther than the modern educational system. With modern education, you go to school, earn a degree, and get a job. The focus is on success and happiness only in this life—beyond that, not so much. The emphasis is on material development only to satisfy the five sense desires; it pays little attention to mental qualities. But still, education is crucial for having material comfort in this life, and it can expose the individual to an expanded range of ideas. In Buddhism, your education is not so limited. Here you are educated in wisdom and compassion to benefit yourself and all other sentient beings, for this life and all future lives until you attain enlightenment and are completely free of duality and suffering. Buddhism offers you the ultimate fulfillment.

The Mahayana and Vajrayana approach to education is systematically categorized into view, meditation, and conduct. The view of Buddhist philosophy is the nature of reality, freedom from duality. Meditation is the method used to approach, understand, and realize that view. Conduct is our proper behavior: avoiding the ten nonvirtues and practicing the ten virtues, which supports one's view and meditation. All the problems in society, in our countries, and in the world come about because of people lack moral ethics or discipline. Everyone everywhere, regardless of their religion or culture, can appreciate someone who maintains good discipline. The ten virtues are the universal source of peace and harmony, while conversely the ten nonvirtues are the universal source of suffering and conflict.

That is what they studied at Nalanda University, a place where hundreds of thousands of great masters were produced. The same teachings are still appreciated and alive today. We are not trying to bring some old, outdated system into the present time. The Buddha's teachings have relevance and usefulness today. Bringing them into our lives is the greatest service to human beings, and to all other sentient beings, that we could perform, as well as the fulfillment of the highest purpose of human life. The purpose of life is to become free from suffering and to bring others real peace and happiness. This is why we must study and practice the Dharma teachings. Even though this physical university was destroyed, its tradition of teachings and wisdom is still alive in the world.

The Great Nalanda Master Shantideva

Shantideva, who lived in the eighth century, was one of the greatest masters ever produced by Nalanda University. He studied the three divisions of the Buddhist teachings, meditated on them, and dedicated his life to their practice. He stayed in a meditative state all the time, day and night, including when he was eating, sleeping, walking, and so on. He engaged very little in the daily activities of the monastery. Some of his fellow monks misunderstood this, and thought that he was a lazy disgrace who should be expelled from the monastery. Their problem was that he hadn't broken any of the rules, so they had to scheme and act indirectly. They asked him to give a public teaching, thinking that he would not be able to do so and would leave Nalanda out of embarrassment.

On the appointed day, Shantideva asked the assembled group what kind of teaching he should give, something old or something that was unknown. The crowd responded that they wanted to hear a teaching that hadn't been given before. Shantideva said he had no special topics that were not taught before, but in order to develop his own practice and to benefit other interested persons, he had written the *Bodhicharyavatara*. They had no idea that he had secretly authored three works. The text of medium length was the *Bodhicharyavatara*, known in English as *Engaging in the Bodhisattva's Way of Life*, which he recited and explained thoroughly. Toward the end, while Shantideva was reciting from the ninth chapter, he rose into the air and disappeared. His voice could still be heard until the text was finished. In the centuries following this event, that book became one of the most revered works in all of Buddhist literature.

Engaging in the Bodhisattva's Way of Life is worthy of our attention. We should study it as much as we can and practice it even more. This book gives so many clear reasons why we need to practice bodhichitta to purify the causes of our suffering, delusion, and negative thoughts. It helps us practice handling these thoughts productively. There are ten chapters in this text, from which I will highlight key teachings below.

1. The Benefits of the Awakening Mind

First, *Engaging in the Bodhisattva's Way of Life* describes the importance of bodhichitta and explains that all the buddhas of the three times attained buddhahood by perfecting bodhichitta. Just as alchemy transforms plain metal to gold, bodhichitta transforms sentient beings into bodhisattvas. Bodhichitta is the source of all the excellent qualities of a buddha. The moment one cultivates bodhichitta, even without having fully purified the mental afflictions, one becomes a source of refuge, hope, and peace. All the peace and happiness that arises throughout the world, all the way to buddhahood, occurs by practicing loving-kindness, compassion, and bodhichitta. Anyone interested in comprehending the suffering of sentient beings, alleviating delusion, and establishing peace and happiness in samsara and nirvana should know that bodhichitta is the direct cause.

2. Disclosure of Wrongdoing

The disclosure of wrongdoing purifies mental obscurations and the mistakes we have made because of them. It purifies whatever karma we have created through negative physical, mental, or verbal actions. As Milarepa taught, it is best not to make a mistake, but if you do, the second best is to confess and purify it. Confess in front of the enlightened beings all the negative acts that you have done physically, mentally, and verbally. Reveal them all, one by one, without reservation. We confess and purify them because they are the causes of the suffering that we do not want. Then after that, resolve not to repeat those actions again. As bodhisattvas, we don't purify just our own negative karma, but the negative karma of every sentient being in samsara. We sincerely wish that all sentient beings become free of delusion and negative actions. We use the Buddha's wisdom and compassion as a cure and remedy to purify our delusions. Nonvirtuous deeds and negative karma are obstacles to the cultivation of bodhichitta, so the more we purify them the better our opportunity to cultivate and practice bodhichitta.

3. Full Acceptance of the Awakening Mind

In this chapter, Shantideva rejoices in all the deeds of enlightened beings, buddhas and bodhisattvas, requests buddhas to turn the wheel of Dharma to dispel ignorance, and requests the buddhas not to pass into parinirvana. He aspires to benefit beings in many different ways, and makes this famous promise:

> As the previous buddhas embraced the enlightened mind
> and progressed on the bodhisattva path,
> I, too, for the benefit of all sentient beings, give birth to
>   bodhichitta
> and apply myself to accomplish the stages of the path.[5]

We, too, should recite this verse and cultivate this universal mind of bodhichitta for all sentient beings.

4. Vigilance

Vigilance and mindfulness are the keys to the accomplishment of bodhichitta practice. Thus, this chapter concerns how to protect bodhichitta and increase it with mindfulness once it has been cultivated. As we protect our own eyes, bodhisattvas should protect bodhichitta, the eye of wisdom. The point of the Buddha's teachings is to attain buddhahood. Once we have cultivated bodhichitta, we must never, ever give it up. No matter what happens to us after we cultivate this precious mind, we must keep it firmly in our hearts. Having grasped bodhichitta, we should not separate from it until we become buddhas ourselves. To do this, we must always remain vigilant and protect precious bodhichitta. From beginningless time until now, many buddhas have taught the Dharma, but we failed to connect with those teachings because of our negative karma. If we don't make progress now, when we finally have a good connection, what hope is there?

5. Guarding Alertness

Next, the text describes moral ethics: how to maintain discipline and how to attain pure conduct by avoiding the ten non-virtues and cherishing the ten virtues. Moral discipline is one of the three higher trainings, the principal instruction in all Buddhist schools. Morality isn't just for monks and nuns, but for everyone who wants happiness. We should keep in mind that no matter who you are—educated, uneducated, rich, or poor—we all need to avoid nonvirtuous thoughts and actions, and pursue virtue. It doesn't matter if you are Buddhist or non-Buddhist because this is the universal law of cause and effect. The second training is meditation. On the basis of morality, it is easier to keep the mind calm, peaceful, and serenely clear. When the mind is peaceful, there is an opportunity for the third training, special insight or wisdom, to arise. These three are interrelated and support each other; they are all required to become free from samsara. We each have the responsibility to protect our mind with these trainings. No one can guard or protect your mind for you.

6. Patience

Shantideva's next practice is patience and, in particular, subduing the unruly mind. Even though none of us wants to be angry or upset, these emotions seem to arise on their own when certain causes and conditions come together. When there is anger in the mind, all peace is destroyed. Even if you are eating a delicious meal in a beautiful place, all that comfort can be destroyed in an instant by anger. The Buddha very clearly taught the purification of anger, rage, resentment, jealousy, and so forth, instead of their suppression. And we *can* purify them by using the steps and many methods that are grounded in the practices of compassion and wisdom.

Consider for a moment how everyone in this world is suffering. There is no one in samsara who does not suffer. Even the most powerful man or the richest woman in the world suffers like everyone else. Think about that and cultivate sincere compassion; reinforce your practice of bodhichitta for everyone equally: for those you know and those you do not know, for those who are friends and those who are enemies. When we develop compassion, negative thoughts will not arise. Make your mind peaceful and joyful. That is the purpose of Dharma practice and of staying on the path. This is not only religious training, but also the way to contain the fire of suffering.

7. Perseverance

The next topic in *Engaging in the Bodhisattva's Way of Life* is perseverance, the joyous effort we must make to study and practice bodhichitta. The Dharma is the one true solution to our delusion and the genuine method to relieve our suffering. Appreciate that, and then progress step by step. Sometimes we feel that we are not good enough or that we do not have enough intelligence, but those are mistaken notions. Since we have buddha nature, there will be definite progress if we make an effort. This has been demonstrated time and again in Buddhist history. Some of the most poor, distraught, and badly behaved people went on to be very successful in the study and practice of Dharma, so much so that they became completely free of samsara. Likewise, we must persevere without attachment to this life or to samsaric activities. Dharma practice is not just for today and is not just for this life. Practice to be free from the entire cycle of samsara. We must use this precious human life in the best way. That is joyous effort. Recognize your good fortune and make the best use of this rare opportunity created by a connection to your previous lives. We are so fortunate—it is like a dream come true! So fully devote your body, speech, and mind to the Buddha, Dharma, and Sangha, and follow the path of bodhichitta with joy and enthusiasm. Study enough to understand the meaning of the Dharma and then practice to experience it personally.

8. Meditation

Meditative absorption helps us bring the mind into the right place. When the mind is very busy, when it scatters and cannot settle down, it is very difficult to purify obscurations and cultivate bodhichitta. To accomplish these things and make the mind peaceful, you must bring it to the right place through meditation. Mindfulness is the key. When you drive, you should drive with mindfulness. When you eat, you should eat with mindfulness. When you do anything, you should examine yourself: What are you doing? What are you thinking? Is it in the right direction or wrong direction from the point of view of the ten virtues and the ten nonvirtues?

Practice meditative concentration in this way. Sit in the morning and sit in the evening, just to observe the mind with meditation. By purifying afflictions, we can achieve a state of meditative absorption in equipoise, which allows the natural clarity and purity of the mind to surface. Mental clarity and purity bring a great opportunity to kindle the light of wisdom and to see the true nature of reality directly. Without mental afflictions, your buddha nature is fully revealed. It is like a sunrise dispelling darkness; the darkness simply disappears in the sunlight. Likewise, when pristine clarity arises, there is no chance for negative thoughts to manifest. They simply disappear. Samadhi is the foundation for the quality of the mind that will kindle incisive wisdom.

9. Wisdom

Shantideva's chapter on wisdom awareness contains a great deal of analysis as well as meditation practices. The practices of generosity, moral ethics, patience, and perseverance are methods to develop the strength of relative bodhichitta and to arouse the wisdom that realizes ultimate bodhichitta. There are many different wisdoms, like the various wisdoms of the world, such as healing, engineering, metaphysics, and languages, and then there is the wisdom that transcends samsara. This latter wisdom is the tool used to alleviate all the ignorance about samsara and nirvana.

We know that everyone in samsara is in a state of hope and fear; we hope to gain and at the same time we fear losing. Wherever we go, our ego clinging is always pushing us to hope and fear. Shantideva's wisdom chapter examines whether there is a self that truly exists. If there is one, then hope and fear would be justified. However, analysis shows that there is no independently existing self. You should conduct this analysis yourself to find out where the self is. Is your hair your self? Is your skin your self? Is your body your self? None of these are the self. Our body is the composite of many causes and conditions, the four elements, consciousness, and so forth. It is just an illusion, like a mirage or a reflection. Due to our ignorance and delusion, we hold on to it as "myself" and "me," and as a result, we suffer helplessly out of attachment and aversion. Consider that understanding and develop compassion for all other sentient beings who suffer from the same thing. Greater compassion will manifest from this transcendent wisdom, and greater wisdom will manifest from this compassion; they support each other.

10. Dedication

At the end of each meditation session we must practice dedication. All the merit and virtue we have gathered must be dedicated to the enlightenment of all sentient beings. Otherwise, it will be wasted on momentary pleasures. Near the end of the text, Shantideva prays:

For as long as space endures
and for as long as living beings remain
until then may I, too, abide
to dispel the misery of the world.[6]

Suppose you received a big piece of gold in a dream. While you are dreaming, the gold and your feeling of happiness seem completely real. But then a dream thief comes and steals that dream gold and you suffer from anger. In the dream, it was all true. You felt happiness when you got the gold, and you were upset and suffered when the gold was taken away. Upon awakening, none of it exists: no gold, no happiness, no anger. Likewise, in samsara, as long as we believe that there is a true self, there is constant suffering caused by hope and fear. The Buddha's teachings are indispensable because without them, there isn't any way to awaken from the dream of samsara and become free from suffering. If you truly want to become free from suffering, study and practice this teaching step by step to purify all your deeply rooted habitual tendencies until you reach enlightenment.

Chanting mantras and praying are good, but they are not enough. We must implant the teachings in our heart. The Kagyü tradition has such a great way of doing this: first you study and practice and then you go into retreat. Both steps are appreciated and emphasized. Because our lineage's great masters, such as Milarepa, Gampopa, and Jigten Sumgön, established this tradition we are able to receive all these precious Dharma teachings. Because of Shantideva's Mahayana tradition of study and practice, our lineage has come through to us. Look at their lives and see how they studied and practiced, and aspire to follow in their footsteps. This is the way to free ourselves from all delusions and achieve complete enlightenment, the perfect state of peace and happiness.

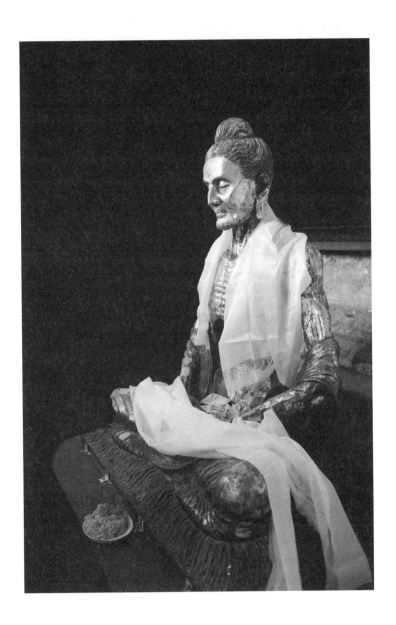

Then the twice-born, who took delight in austerities,
described in due order to the bull of the Shakyas,
a very bull in prowess,
their particularities and the fruit thereof:

"Uncultivated food, that which grows in the water,
leaves, water, fruit and also roots,
this is what the sages live on in accordance with the scriptures;
but there are various separate alternatives.

"Some live like the birds by what they can pick up from the ground,
others graze on grass like the deer,
and others pass their time with the snakes,
or turned into anthills by the forest wind.

"Some gain their subsistence by laborious pounding with stones,
others eat only what has been husked by their own teeth,
and some again cook for others
and meet their needs with anything that may be left over.

"Some with their coils of matted hair soaked with water
twice offer oblations to Agni with sacred texts;
others plunge into the water and dwell with the fishes,
their bodies scored by turtles.

"With such austerities accumulated for the due time,
the higher win Paradise, and the lower enter the world of men.
For bliss is obtained by the path of suffering;
for bliss, they say, is the ultimate end of dharma."

The child of the lord of men listened to these
and like statements of the anchorites.
Though he had not yet reached the perception of reality,
He was not satisfied.
—Ashvagosha, *Buddhacarita*

CHAPTER 6

Mahakala's Cave: Skillful Means

UP A STEEP SLOPE from the banks of the Phalgu River about seven miles northeast of Bodh Gaya, a set of three shallow caves stands halfway up a rocky bluff. This is believed to be the site at which the Buddha engaged in severe ascetic practices for six years before his awakening, although this is unconfirmed by archaeological evidence. It is only in the past hundred years or so that archaeologists have rediscovered and identified the holy places of India. But for a pilgrim, the scientifically precise location is not so important as the devotion that a place inspires. The Buddha walked all around this region, so in actuality every place is holy.

Near the entrance to the caves are a small Tibetan Buddhist monastery and a stupa, both built in recent years. After passing through a low and narrow doorway, a golden statue depicting the emaciated buddha-to-be can be seen in one small cave; a large, more conventional Buddha statue stands in another. A shrine honoring the Hindu goddess Dungeshwari is also located here, so this site is sometimes called the Dungeshwari Cave Temples. It is more widely known as the Mahakala Cave, memorializing a great Vajrayana practitioner named

Mahasiddha Shavaripa who practiced Six-Armed Mahakala, the wrathful form of Avalokiteshvara, here. The yogi meditated in this cave for many years, and eventually experienced a vision of Six-Armed Mahakala.

We come to the sacred places of the Buddha, of bodhisattvas, and of great Dharma practitioners to remind ourselves to be without regard for samsara. Thus, it is very important to relax the mind while visiting or contemplating these holy places. Samsara should be perceived only as a state of confusion and suffering. Leave samsaric matters behind; bring the mind to bodhichitta. Purify your dualistic thoughts and afflicting emotions. Bring the mind to the right place. Appreciate, rejoice, and feel fortunate that you have an opportunity to progress toward enlightenment.

Skillful Means in Vajrayana

In the Vajrayana tradition we find deities with a variety of expressions. Some are serene and beautiful and some, like Mahakala, are wrathful and frightening. People can be confused by this and wonder how holy deities can have fangs and display threatening weapons. Among sentient beings we can find infinite combinations of mental delusion and affliction. Many, but not all, of them can be purified through peaceful means. These preexisting propensities began a long time ago, and they need to be handled skillfully. Accordingly, there are different methods of addressing them, commonly categorized into four activities: peaceful, increasing, magnetizing, and wrathful. These methods are designed to counter all our mental afflictions.

We can successively apply these four activities to our own

mind. First, based on wisdom and compassion, we peacefully observe our mental obscurations in our meditation practice. Once we have established a state of peaceful meditation, we expand the power of our meditation to control our afflicting emotions with wisdom and compassion, using our understanding of emptiness. These are the increasing and magnetizing activities. But this may not be enough to completely eliminate the afflictions. We have become accustomed to delusions for such a long time that it is very difficult to get rid of them. Even though we know intellectually that they are just empty illusions, they stubbornly remain within our mindstream and push and lead us in the wrong direction very easily. In that case, your wisdom and compassion need more power, more strength, and more courage to forcefully expel them. It is this concept of fierce strength that the wrathful deities express.

Since the Buddha was enlightened, he would have perfected all the skills for working with the mind in order to help sentient beings. Therefore, we must develop the same skills and methods to purify all our mental obscurations, step by step. Using just one method is not enough, just as one medicine is not enough to cure all diseases. As long as any delusion remains, we cannot expect genuine peace and happiness. Thus, to purify *all* the causes of suffering, we need to apply *all* the different methods.

The Buddha and the Robber

No matter what nonvirtuous deeds you may have committed in the past, with skillful means, they can be overcome and left behind. There is a wonderful story that demonstrates how the

Buddha was able to skillfully turn a dangerous robber from a life of crime to that of an exemplary practitioner:

There was a robber in a desolate place who ruthlessly attacked everyone he met; no one could escape from his hand. One day he met the Buddha but did not know who he was. He stopped the Buddha and told him that no one could escape without being either robbed or killed. Without any fear, Buddha stood before him and said, "Okay, but before you kill me, I have two questions that I would like to ask you."

The robber said, "What are they?"

Pointing to a big tree nearby, the Buddha said, "Can you bring down all the leaves of that tree?" Of course, the robber was young and strong, and he had a very sharp knife. He was eager to show off his strength, so he cut down all the leaves in a short time. The Buddha admitted that this display was very impressive, and that the robber was indeed very strong.

When the robber asked for the second question, the Buddha asked whether he could put all the leaves back. "How can you ask such a question?" exclaimed the robber, shocked.

The Buddha replied, "Why not? Since you could bring the leaves down so easily, why wouldn't you be able to put them back?" The robber was embarrassed and intimidated; he was so confused that he forgot to kill the Buddha. The Buddha took this opportunity to say, "Think about how many people you have robbed and killed with ease. You brought down all the leaves the same way, but now it is hard to put them back. How much peace and happiness have you brought to others? It is easy to destroy others' peace and happiness but very difficult to give them. Suppose a stronger man came here and told you that he intended to kill you. Look at your mind—how would you feel? If someone else came along and protected you, how much would you appreciate it and rejoice?" The robber felt great remorse when he reflected on what he had done in the past. He had caused so much suffering to so many people, and he had not given aid to anyone.

Standing in front of the Buddha, who had such profound wisdom, completely changed his mind. The robber admitted, "Yes, I have made a big mistake. From today on, I will give up all these bad actions. I want to follow you, and I want to study and practice."

The Buddha's compassion and wisdom skillfully helped that robber who had such a deluded mind. The Buddha could have frustrated the robber by flying up into the sky to escape or he could have knocked the robber down with his power. But the Buddha did not do that—he just used skillful methods that anyone could have used. This demonstrates how the Buddha can help lead others to freedom from delusion and suffering.

Following in the Buddha's Footsteps

Those of us who are not enlightened can still follow in the Buddha's footsteps and use his enlightened methods. Regardless of our wealth, gender, social status, or race, we all have an opportunity to reflect on samsara and the causes of suffering, and then refrain from creating the causes of suffering. We can all aspire to follow in the steps of the Buddha, who showed the path for everyone equally with wisdom and compassion. All we need is our interest. Practice joyfully with appreciation for the path that eliminates all the causes of suffering.

When we spend long hours chanting mantras or saying prayers, we may feel that there is not much progress. Then we wonder, What went wrong? What is happening? Maybe we think that the Dharma is not working. The Dharma works! We just have to know how to implement it. Therefore, we need courage, dedication, determination, and understanding. There is no alternative; there is no other way. We must encourage ourselves to persevere and continue forward on the path. This is the way that allows us to free ourselves from suffering by taking care of its causes and conditions. Instead of focusing on high expectations about buddhahood, we should learn how to deal with the root causes of suffering.

Everyone has buddha nature, the effulgent seed of enlightenment. We know this because, by nature, every being has some kind of love and compassion; even small insects and vicious predators care for their young. That awareness of love and compassion is a reflection of buddha nature. Buddha nature is total peace, full of luminosity. From this innate mind, the desire to be free from suffering and to achieve peace and happiness is ever present. This characteristic will never change, however or wherever you are reborn, even as an insect or in the hell realm. Only those who have consciousness, meaning they have a mind, have buddha nature. A rock or plant doesn't have that kind of awareness; it doesn't have buddha nature, the fundamental basis for enlightenment.

However, we also need a precious human life as a support and working basis for enlightenment. A "precious" human life is one that is both rare and useful, and enjoys the qualities of the eight leisures and ten endowments (see glossary of enumerations). Among all the six realms, it is a precious human life that is the best foundation for exercising this potential of the mind. On the foundation of a precious human life, from the seed of compassion and awareness, we expand this potential infinitely to all sentient beings. We expand that awareness and knowledge to all sentient beings in samsara and nirvana. Then we can have an opportunity to purify all our obscurations, one step at a time. When buddha nature is fully revealed and we can see it precisely, nothing is hidden. Then we can say, "I am free from all suffering." We can achieve that within in our own being. Therefore, we each need to have the responsibility and dedication to go forward until the ultimate goal, buddhahood, is realized. Until then, the clarity of the mind's effulgence will remain obscured by our delusion.

When buddhas and bodhisattvas train perfectly in bodhichitta, they develop every skill, type of wisdom, compassionate action, and ability to help sentient beings without limit. Through many different ways and avenues, the Buddha and great bodhisattvas benefit sentient beings in whatever way is required, whether it be wrathful or peaceful or in between. Even though buddhas and bodhisattvas have the ability to benefit others, interdependence is still at work. They can only reach those who are interested and have devotion.

The sage, whose every effort was pure
and who delighted in a lonely habitation,
took up His dwelling on the pure bank of the Nairanjanā River. [. . .]

He undertook extraordinary austerities by starvation,
thinking that that must be the method
for ending death and rebirth. [. . .]

The sage, whose body was being tormented
to no purpose by pernicious austerities, thus resolved:
"This is not the way of life for passionlessness, for enlightenment,
    for liberation.
How can the result to be attained by the mind
be reached by a man who is not calmly at ease
and who is so worn out with the exhaustion of hunger and thirst
that his mind is unbalanced by that exhaustion?" [. . .]

At that time, by divine instigation, the daughter of the cowherd chief
went there, joy bursting from her heart.
Doing obeisance with her head,
she caused him to accept milk rice.
—Ashvagosha, *Buddhacarita*

CHAPTER 7

Sujata's Tree: Meditation Instructions

THE PHALGU RIVER, known in the Buddha's time as the Nairanjana, flows just to the east of the main entrance to the Mahabodhi Temple area. On its far side stand monuments associated with the story of the maid Sujata: a commemorative brick stupa built in the fifth century, a set of more recent statues placed on an ancient base that depicts the historical event said to have taken place there, a tree understood to mark the exact spot where Sujata offered food to the future Buddha, and the remains of several other monuments and statues from ancient times. The area has not received much attention from archaeologists and is relatively unrestored.

Nonetheless, this site marks one of the more significant events in the Buddha's life. Following the religious practices of his time, he had spent six years in extreme physical deprivation prior to his enlightenment. Some sources record that he subsisted on a daily grain of rice and a sesame seed while living in various forests and caves. At this tree near the Nairanjana River, he reached a crossroad. Being weak and miserable had brought him no closer to enlightenment; something had to change. A local girl who tended milk cows saw the starving stranger and did what came naturally to her—she offered him a bowl of rice soaked in milk. In a pivotal moment, the future Buddha accepted the food and abandoned his former ascetic practices. The five monks accompanying him were dismayed at what they saw as his lax discipline and summarily abandoned him. As we know, Siddhartha Gotama proceeded to walk a short way; seat himself on the vajrasana, the seat of enlightenment; and begin his final meditations. Thus, it is most appropriate for us to use the site of Sujata's offering as inspiration to deepen our own meditation practice.

Meditation

First, just reflect, and appreciate that you have a precious human life. Because of this precious human body, you have a special gift, a mind that is interested in the Buddha, Dharma, and Sangha. You have developed devotion, and now you are so fortunate to have this great opportunity to learn about the holy places of the Buddha's lifetime. Whether or not you follow in his literal footsteps in India, you are following his path to escape samsara, the vicious cycle of suffering. So, deeply rejoice and feel how fortunate you are. Turn your mind to the Dharma and relax.

When you undertake serious meditation, perhaps engaging in long sessions for many days, it is important to sit in a good position. First, the body should be straight but not tense. Relax and expand the shoulders so they are not tight. Legs and feet cross in the lotus or half-lotus position. Hands rest on the lap, palms facing upward, right over left, with the thumb tips touching. The neck bends slightly forward. The eyes gaze downward, looking neither too far away nor too close. Place the tip of the tongue against the roof of the mouth, just behind the front teeth. Leave the jaw in a natural position, not wide open and not closed tight. This is how to relax physically.

Now take a deep breath and fill your entire body with air. Release all your physical and mental tension. Breathe in and out all the way down to the navel. Meditate with your mind inseparable from the breath. Let all your various thoughts dissolve into emptiness. Imagine the Buddha meditating, calming his mind into equipoise, resting in the nature of space. We can do the same.

First reflect on impermanence. Everything—all composite phenomena in the world and the sentient beings within it—is based on many causes and conditions and is constantly changing. Observing the four seasons, day and night, and the passing of every second makes this very obvious and clear. When a child grows into a young person who then becomes old, when the poor become rich, or when the rich become poor, it is all just a play of impermanence. The beautiful flower fades, rainbows disappear; meditate on this. Release attachment to persons, wealth, and status. Reflect and take a deep breath. The Buddha taught this method to free us from suffering, so we should practice it with enthusiasm and a grateful heart.

Relax the mind and develop loving-kindness for all beings—humans, animals, birds, sea mammals, and insects. They all want the same peace and happiness that you do, but they must endure mental and physical suffering. The rich and the poor, young and old, our friends and enemies, even those who are very capable—none are free from suffering. See this precisely and let compassion develop. Sometimes, gaze at the sky and meditate on compassion. Sometimes, gaze at the sea and meditate on compassion. Relax your muscles and free your mind from delusions.

After this, meditate on bodhichitta, the only way to achieve buddhahood. Relative bodhichitta is the practice of aspiring to attain buddhahood for the benefit of all sentient beings. Action bodhichitta is the purification of nonvirtuous thoughts and actions by practicing the six *paramitas*, or perfections. To reinforce your bodhichitta, take refuge in the Buddha, Dharma, and Sangha. In doing so, you rely on the guidance of the great bodhisattvas who have come before you, and you depend on the Buddha's wisdom and compassion. This is not religious training; rather, it is a special method to release delusion and enhance one's clarity of mind.

Next, look at the arising thoughts and investigate where they come from. When a thought dissolves, watch it carefully. Where does it go? You cannot find any specific place from which thoughts originate or into which they dissipate. Without chasing the thought, rest the mind. For just a few moments, put down this book and relax. Allow yourself to be where you are. The past is gone, and the future has not yet come. This moment is like a ripple in water. Like a rainbow, it looks vivid but has no essence. All sounds are like echoes without substance. Some may praise you and others may show you contempt. All of this is nothing more than echoing noise.

Thoughts manifest in the mind like clouds manifest in the sky. Where do the clouds come from? Although they appear in the sky, there is no special source of clouds. Likewise, in our mind, thoughts arise from nowhere. They are merely an illusion. Let them dissolve. After clouds appear in the sky they dissolve into space, leaving no trace. Observe the mind when thoughts arise; they arise from emptiness and they dissolve into emptiness. They leave no trace unless we grasp or fixate on them. When we follow negative thoughts such as attachment, desire, anger, aversion, or jealousy, they surround us with confusion and suffering. If, instead, we were to recall that they are illusory, dependent on causes and conditions, they would have no ability to function. As soon as we know that the absence of a single cause or condition will destroy that negative thought, they disappear into emptiness. This is how to use wisdom to break down our long-standing habit of ignorance. Don't think that you can accomplish this in one or two meditation sessions. It may take an entire lifetime to deconstruct your delusions.

Take some time to inhale deeply and exhale fully. Look at your thoughts and find that they do not exist anywhere. We are not making them empty; their very nature is emptiness. We need vigilance, mindfulness, and courage to see that delusions are contrived fabrications. Our own nature itself is peace and happiness. Rest the mind in that state for as long as you are able.

We do not meditate merely to escape our immediate suffering or to unwind from stress. Things done for this life, whether that's meditating or earning titles, are all left behind when we go on to the next cycle of samsara. As Buddhists, our goal is much broader—it is the enlightenment of all sentient beings. We dare not waste this precious human life on selfishness. We reflect on the whole of samsara and follow the footsteps of the Buddha on the path to buddhahood, the ultimate solution to all suffering. We need a very farsighted view, one that is concerned not only for ourselves, but all others as well. We develop wisdom, insight, and compassion so that we understand how to tackle the root cause of all this unwanted suffering and bring the vicious cycles of confusion to an end.

We must practice this method repeatedly because we are so firmly habituated in mental delusion and affliction. These inveterate propensities have existed throughout countless lifetimes, so we feel natural and comfortable when delusions manifest. When we try to eliminate them, our efforts feel artificial and we despair that the task is impossible. Consider how hard it is to break a habit like smoking cigarettes or drinking alcohol. The process can be quite painful and difficult. Still, with enough interest, determination, and skill, one can overcome such habits and have a better life. Likewise, dismantling our delusion habit requires many skills and methods. First, we must be convinced that it is possible and necessary to rid ourselves of the adventitious defilements. Reflecting on the impermanence of all composite phenomena, understanding the various layers of physical and mental suffering and their causes, trusting in the infallible nature of karma, practicing loving-kindness and compassion, cultivating bodhichitta, and experiencing the empty nature of all phenomena—all these skills and methods will help make our meditation practice productive. Practice without expectation or fear. If we can do this in our day-to-day life, there is no doubt that the desired result will manifest, because we will have created its cause.

Resplendent with power and glory,
He came shining like the sun to the Deer Park,
where dwelt the great seers among trees
resounding with cuckoos' calls.

Then the five mendicants—
he of the Kaundinya gotra, Mahanaman, Vaspa, Asvajit,
    and Bhadrajit—
seeing Him from afar,
spoke these words among themselves:

"Here approaches the mendicant Gotama,
who in his fondness for ease has turned away from asceticism.
He is certainly not to be met, not to be saluted;
for one who has retreated from his vow merits no reverence.
Should he, however, wish to talk with us,
by all means enter into conversation with him,
for men of gentle blood should certainly do so,
whoever may be the guest who arrives."

The Buddha moved toward the sitting mendicants,
who had thus laid their plans,
and as He drew nearer to them,
they broke their agreement. [. . .]

The mendicants displayed their skepticism
regarding the truth to the Tathagata.
The Knower of the Path, knowing the path to enlightenment
    to be other than theirs,
expounded the path to them.
—Ashvagosha, *Buddhacarita*

CHAPTER 8

Sarnath: The Four Noble Truths

WE FIND THAT Sarnath is little changed from ancient times in many ways. A famous deer sanctuary was there in the Buddha's time, and one remains there today. In fact, the name Sarnath derives from a legend associated with the Buddha, who in a previous lifetime gave his life to save the life of a pregnant doe. This is the place to which the Buddha walked after he achieved enlightenment. Here, he reunited with the five companions who had deserted him at Sujata's tree; gave his first, second, and third Dharma teachings; and spent his first rainy season in retreat.

Just outside the grounds of the archaeological site is the Chaukhandi Stupa, traditionally said to mark the spot where the Buddha reunited with his five companions. The Dharmarajika Stupa was destroyed in the 1700s to provide materials for a building project in Varanasi. Only the foundation remains, but it is popularly regarded as the site of the first Dharma teaching, that of the four noble truths. The most striking and most complete monument here is the circular Dhamekh Stupa, traditionally said to be the site of the second teaching, that of the *Anatmalakshana Sutra*, which teaches the characteristics of nonself. Adjacent to the archaeological site stands a modern temple that was constructed by the Maha Bodhi Society to commemorate the Mulagandhakuti (Greatly Fragrant Hut) where the Buddha resided during the first rainy season following his enlightenment. It is also the place from which he dispersed his early disciples to spread the Dharma throughout the countryside. In later years, the Buddha returned here to teach several times.

The primary reason that Sarnath has inspired Buddhists for millennia is because this is where the Buddha set the wheel of Dharma in motion—in other words, where he first explained the nature of samsara and the path to enlightenment. The Buddha himself said that the sight of Sarnath would arouse devotion in his followers after he had passed away. So many people visit the holy places of the Buddha. Some are rich, some are poor; some are educated, some are uneducated. They all come to pay respect to the Buddha and his teachings because they desire peace and happiness. Whether their goal is finding happiness in this life or attaining enlightenment, their motivation is to stop suffering. All the undesirable suffering in the world comes from negative thoughts and negative actions, whereas all peace and happiness in world come from positive thoughts and positive actions. This is not just a belief, but the reality that the Buddha revealed. This is the empirical nature of all phenomena; it is simply the way things work.

The Four Noble Truths

Before he became a buddha, Prince Siddhartha happened to witness different types of suffering. This inspired him to investigate what suffering really is and what causes it. He searched and meditated for six years, culminating in his enlightenment at Bodh Gaya. Afterward, he hesitated to share his new understanding, thinking that no one would be able to understand it. But eventually he went to Sarnath and reunited with his five former companions. The five ascetic monks requested repeatedly that he turn the wheel of Dharma, that he share the unafflicted ambrosia he had found. So, he taught the wisdom he had gained to his five companions and many great bodhisattvas who had gathered to listen. We call this first teaching the four noble truths, or sometimes the four truths of the noble ones. "Noble" here indicates that the truth he spoke is that which is perceived by an enlightened being, not the mistaken view that a confused mind usually understands.

The Buddha said that because we have not understood the four noble truths, we have been in samsara for a long time. Once we understand them, we will be free from the vicious cycle of suffering. With that statement, he started to teach the four noble truths:

1. The noble truth of suffering
2. The noble truth of the origin of suffering
3. The noble truth of the cessation of suffering
4. The noble truth of the path to cessation

In terms of causality, the first two are the cause of samsara and the second two are the cause of nirvana. The cause of samsara is karma and the afflicting emotions, and the result is the suffering of the three realms. The cause of nirvana is the thirty-seven factors of enlightenment, which include the eightfold path, and the result is the truth of cessation. To explain by example, suffering is like a physical sickness, where the cause is identified by a doctor. Recovering from the sickness is the cessation of suffering, and the prescription of the cure is the eightfold path.

Once you know about suffering, there is nothing more to know. Once you have abandoned the cause of suffering, there is nothing more to abandon. Once you have attained cessation of suffering, there is nothing more to attain. Once you have followed the path, there is nothing more to follow. This is the comprehensive way to understand the four noble truths. We will look briefly at each of the four in order.

The Truth of Suffering

In order to free ourselves from suffering, it is important for us to work with a deeper meaning of suffering, not with just a superficial understanding. First, we must recognize suffering and understand it in its three forms:

1. the suffering of suffering,
2. the suffering of change, and
3. pervasive or conditioned suffering.

Generally, of these forms of suffering, beings in the three lower realms experience more suffering of suffering. Human beings, demigods, and gods have more suffering of change, and those in the form and formless realms have more conditioned suffering. But as we will see, any being in samsara is subject to these three forms of suffering.

We are all familiar with the suffering of suffering. This is suffering that is physical or mental, and is something that even small insects can recognize. As for physical suffering, we get old, we get sick, and finally we die. We get cold, hot, tired, hungry, and so forth. Mentally, we suffer when we get what we do not want and when we cannot get what we desire, as well as when we lose our loved ones and meet enemies. Of course, there are many other kinds of mental and physical suffering; these are just a few examples. We do not learn about the various types of suffering and impermanence to scare ourselves, but to be reminded of where we are. Ignoring the fact that we are in samsara doesn't help us find a solution. Only when we see things realistically do we gain an opportunity to find a solution, to discover and eliminate the cause of these unwanted consequences. We are so fortunate to have the wisdom of the Buddha's teachings to provide a means to overcome our shortcomings and uproot our mental delusions. We should take full advantage to see suffering thoroughly and achieve total enlightenment, which means total freedom from suffering.

When the Buddha said that we should recognize suffering, he meant us to understand the more subtle forms of it, too. The second form is the suffering of change. All the peace, happiness, and joy that we seek and create within samsara will not last for long. They are all subject to change. Everything is impermanent, temporary, changing every moment. This is not just a made-up belief, this is reality. All these changes take place according to causes we have created. Suppose you experience a moment of pleasure, and then suddenly some afflictions manifest in your mind. Everything changes to suffering, doesn't it? That very joy that you experienced has disappeared and you are left feeling terrible. All that happiness vanishes in an instant. We human beings have the mind to understand this. The Dharma teaches us not to attach to fleeting pleasures.

For example, I first came to Sarnath in 1967 as a young and vigorous monk ready to study the Buddha's teachings and philosophy for nine years. Since then, much has changed in the area and in myself. The town is growing and improving and I am getting old. This demonstrates so clearly that nothing stays the same, that the reality we rely on is as illusory as a dream, shifting every moment. When we understand and accept this, we can look into our mind and see that our mental afflictions—our ignorance, our attachment, and our anger—are what create suffering. So let these mental delusions dissolve into impermanence and emptiness. This is why reflecting on impermanence is especially important. If we do not change our mental afflictions, they will continue to create endless suffering for us.

Physically, we change continuously. When we are young, our bodies are strong and firm and we feel like we can do anything. Our faces look beautiful. Then when we become old, we get wrinkled faces and gray hair. We may dye our hair and undergo plastic surgery, but those are very temporary solutions. We might even become depressed and overly focused on our new limitations. What should we do? We must understand impermanence and let go of attachment, hatred, and ignorance. Replace those negative thoughts with contentment and rejoice: "I am so fortunate to have received this Dharma teaching in my life." Meditating on the suffering of change will give you a great opportunity to bring your mind to the right place, meaning not indulging in the causes of suffering. You will find peace and happiness without having to search for them there within you. This can help us develop wisdom and compassion for all those who are going through these sufferings. Practice seeing everything as mirages and bubbles, and experience nonattachment.

The third kind of suffering is pervasive, or conditioned, suffering. As long as we have mental afflictions and karma, we will live within conditioned suffering no matter what we do or where we go. No matter how powerful you are, how rich you may be, how much success you have achieved, even if you've attained the form or formless realm, you will still live with conditioned suffering as long as you still have karma and mental afflictions. The Buddha taught us that we should recognize suffering. This is why. When we get sick, we can use medicine. Material wealth can give us physical comfort. With different technologies and sciences, we can produce extraordinary things; we could even use them to go to Mars. Still, none of this can free us from conditioned suffering. For that, we need the Dharma. This is not just a belief, this is the nature of reality.

The Truth of the Origin of Suffering

Once we understand the different types of suffering we should investigate their causes and do everything we can to avoid them. None of us wants to suffer, yet suffering manifests in every aspect of our lives. How does this happen? Afflictions come from the three poisons—ignorance, attachment, and aversion. When the three poisons arise, they create suffering. Because of ignorance, attachment manifests when we encounter something that we like. Anger manifests when we encounter something that we do not like. Carefully examine these afflicting emotions and you will find that they are nothing more than delusions. There is nothing independent in their nature; they always depend on something else. We are not *always* angry at somebody; we are not *always* attached to something; these thoughts and feelings are momentary. But when we have attachment, anger, jealousy, or pride, there is always suffering. We have every opportunity and means to handle them, and thus avoid creating the causes of more suffering. But once karma is created, we have no choice but to experience suffering.

The Truth of the Cessation of Suffering

Thoughts are made manifest when we put them into action physically or verbally, creating karma. Do you see how we act out of ignorance and how all these emotions are interrelated? If we use our wisdom, our awareness, to look at their nature, we can see that they do not exist anywhere. They are just a habit, albeit a deeply rooted negative habit. Afflicting emotions do not exist independently. It is only due to our habit and our individual pernicious tendencies that they manifest. So if you focus your energy and awareness on them, they lose the power to function. When they do not function, suffering ends, and nirvana is possible. This is the truth of cessation: that the end of suffering is possible.

The Truth of the Path to Cessation

To achieve the cessation of suffering, we must follow the noble eightfold path, which consists of right view, right speech, right thought, right livelihood, right action, right effort, right mindfulness, and right meditative equipoise. These eight have always been the cause of peace and happiness for oneself and for others, and remain so in our time. In ignorance, we keep busy in our lives without any understanding of what actually causes happiness and what causes suffering. Now, thanks to the Buddha's wisdom and compassion, we know how to conduct ourselves productively.

Right view means having a clear mind free of delusion and negative thoughts. When we apply right view, delusion is dispelled. With the right view we cultivate a positive outlook based on wisdom and compassion. It is the realization of emptiness.

On this basis, we engage in *right speech*, which means that we speak truthfully and do not deceive others. These practices give us the opportunity to uproot negative karma.

Right thought means that we cultivate positive thoughts based on compassion and wisdom. Awareness of emptiness and understanding causality and their inseparable nature purifies all the afflicting emotions.

Right livelihood means to live our life without harming others. We all need peace and happiness, and if we harm others we will receive the future result of being harmed.

Right action means to practice the ten virtues and avoid the ten nonvirtues.

Right effort means to work toward purifying negativity and encourage positive actions. We have kept our negative habits for many lifetimes, so it is easy for us to fall back to the negative side and it is difficult for us to sustain a positive state of mind. Therefore, we must keep making an effort to purify all the negative mental, physical, and verbal actions, and to develop all positive actions—not just for this life, but to be freed from samsara.

Right mindfulness means that we keep our mind focused on virtue. Whether we are eating, sleeping, walking, working, or meditating, at every moment and in every place, we always watch our mind with awareness.

Last is *right meditative equipoise*, which means properly calming and stabilizing the mind in a state free from any negative thoughts. When the mind is calm and peaceful, special awareness will develop. Deep within the mind we can precisely understand suffering, the causes of suffering, the possibility of the cessation of suffering, and the path to achieve happiness. The mind is not just one single thing; it has layers upon layers. It takes a long time to work through them all. Meditation practice is the only way to comprehend all the complexities of our delusions and reveal all the enlightened qualities.

This is very brief introduction into four noble truths, which form the framework for all of the Buddha's teachings. All the different levels and paths discussed in the Theravada, Mahayana, and Vajrayana traditions and all the practices that we do are based on this framework. It shows us how to become free from delusion, how to develop insight, and how to achieve the arhat state or even buddhahood.

The Three Higher Trainings

As mentioned earlier, the three higher trainings are the principal instruction that is common to all Buddhist schools. This framework of the path to buddhahood is rooted directly in the four noble truths.

The first training, *shila* in Sanskrit, is moral discipline or pure conduct. This is the discipline of keeping the five precepts for laypeople—abstaining from killing, consuming intoxicants, sexual misconduct, stealing, and wrong speech—as well as additional precepts for monks and nuns. Following the precepts will protect your own peace and happiness, and will keep you from creating more suffering. Individuals who keep them will have a peaceful life, and be widely admired and respected. Even if they are not Buddhist, they are recognized as genuine and trustworthy people. If great numbers of people were to keep these precepts, it would make every country, every society in the world peaceful. Those who do not follow them, but engage in nonvirtuous activities instead, face increased suffering, confusion, and violence. The Buddha had the incomparable wisdom and compassion to show us this path. The wise will look at what the Buddha taught, recognize its universal value, and respect his teachings.

The second training is *samadhi*, or meditative concentration, which means bringing the mind under control and calming it. To watch the mind, you have to look inside. Mind cannot be watched by taking drugs or through physical activity. Mind can only be watched by meditating with compassion and loving-kindness. Watch the mind, relax, and develop the right thoughts. On that basis, establish samadhi step by step: the nine levels in the desire world, the four steps in the form world, and four in the formless realm (see the complete list in appendix C). On the basis of this meditative state of equipoise and mindfulness, we then develop love, compassion, and bodhichitta.

The third training is *prajna*, which translates to "wisdom awareness" or "special insight." Wisdom awareness manifests within the framework of meditative concentration and with the support of moral conduct. When the mind is calm and peaceful, an opportunity to see clearly and precisely is created. When you are angry, you cannot practice bodhichitta, and when you have strong desire and attachment, you cannot practice bodhichitta either. But when your mind is calm and peaceful, you can see what is right and what is wrong for yourself and others—and for enlightenment. When the mind is totally at peace and in equipoise, the light of wisdom can arise within it. All the delusions can be purified. Within the combination of meditative equipoise and special insight, ignorance can be completely purified and self-grasping can be uprooted. This is the only method that can eliminate the third type of suffering, pervasive suffering.

Whether expressed as the four noble truths or the three higher trainings, these are the foundations for our development on the path to free ourselves from suffering. Follow them with discipline and sincere practice, establish your mind in bodhichitta, and then practice Vajrayana by receiving initiations, liberation instructions, and so forth. Until we achieve enlightenment, these teachings help us live our everyday life more peacefully and more compassionately. Therefore, we have a good reason to appreciate the Buddha, to respect him, and develop devotion to him. Rejoicing in his teachings will encourage us to study and practice the Dharma more and more. If you read the histories of great masters, you will see that they all received this same teaching, became thoroughly devoted to it, and attained complete peace and happiness. If you, too, want to become totally free from suffering and have ultimate peace and happiness, this is the only way. This wisdom and these methods are indispensable to bringing peace to every corner of the world.

Thus have I heard. At one time, the Buddha was staying at Kushinagara in the land of the Mallas, close to the river Aji-tavati, where the twin sal trees stood. At that time, the great bhikshus, as many as 80 billion hundred thousand, were with the Blessed One. They surrounded him front and back. On the 15th of the second month, as the Buddha was about to enter Nirvana, he, with his divine power, spoke in a great voice, which filled the whole world and reached the highest of the heavens. It said to all beings in a way each could understand: "Today, the Tathagata, the Alms-deserving and Perfectly Awakened One, pities, protects and, with an undivided mind, sees beings as he does his [son] Rahula. So, he is the refuge and house of the world. The greatly Awakened Blessed One is about to enter Nirvana. Beings who have doubts may all now put questions to him."

Then the Blessed One addressed the brethren, and said, "Behold now, brethren, I exhort you, saying, "Decay is inherent in all component things! Work out your salvation with diligence!" This was the last word of the Tathagata.
—Mahaparinibbana Sutra

CHAPTER 9
Kushinagar: Bodhichitta

KUSHINAGAR is a somber place, reminding us of the parinirvana of the Buddha. The site was abandoned in the 1200s due to invading armies, and forgotten until it was recovered by British archaeologists in the mid-1800s. Today, the most visited spot is the large statue of the dying Buddha reclining on his right side, with his head to the north. The statue was placed there by the devout monk Haribala in the mid-400s. The statue lies inside the Parinirvana Temple, which was built in 1956 but modeled after an ancient temple at Ellora. Just behind the temple is the Parinirvana Stupa, said to mark the actual location of the Buddha's parinirvana. About a mile away is the Ramabhar Stupa, commemorating the site at which the Buddha was cremated. The Matha Kuar Shrine near the Ramabhar Stupa houses a large statue of the seated Buddha that dates from the eleventh century. The ruins of several ancient monasteries and stupas are scattered around the area, as are various modern temples and a museum.

Against Ananda's objections that Kushinagar was too insignificant a place for a buddha to pass away, the Buddha chose it to honor a faithful king from the distant past. After reviewing his teachings, the Buddha asked the assembled disciples whether they had any lingering doubts or questions. None answered, so he gave his final instruction and passed into parinirvana. The local townspeople prepared for his cremation for seven days, but when the time came the funeral pyre would not light. Finally, the great sage Mahakashyapa arrived, and the fire lit spontaneously. The remains were divided among eight kingdoms, each of which erected a stupa to house the precious relics. Only the locations of five of the original great stupas are known. Later, King Ashoka redistributed the relics throughout his kingdom so that devotees could honor them more widely.

The Buddha was born in Lumbini, was raised in Kapilavastu, and became enlightened in Bodh Gaya. He turned the wheel of Dharma first in Sarnath, second in Vulture Peak, and third in Vaishali, and finally passed into parinirvana in Kushinagar. Throughout his lifetime, he performed activities only to benefit sentient beings—not to pass on a cultural tradition or religious belief, but out of wisdom and compassion based on causality. His message of wisdom and compassion has been passed down for generations because it is relevant to everyone who takes an interest. It spread throughout Asia and has continued to take root all over the world. The Buddha's system of study and practice is not "one size fits all." Because the mind has many layers and beings have varied dispositions and capacities, the Buddha taught in a variety of ways to accommodate a wide array of people. This is what allowed his teaching to spread so far and last so long. These profound and vast teachings manifested from the perfection of bodhichitta, from wisdom and compassion.

We should remind ourselves how fortunate we are to have

an opportunity to learn about these holy places. At one time the Buddha stayed in all these places, then great masters followed, but now only ruins remain. The outer appearances—the monasteries, temples, and so forth—were built and destroyed, lost and recovered, but the Buddha's message of wisdom and compassion has never faltered. From this we should learn how important it is for us to study and practice enough to pass the Dharma down to future generations based on our own bodhichitta.

We are interested in learning about these holy places and receiving teachings because we have a precious human life, because of our great virtuous deeds, and because of our devotion to the Buddha, Dharma, and Sangha. This has not happened without a cause or with an incomplete cause. This could only have happened because complete causes and conditions came together through the practice of bodhichitta in our former lives. Since we now have this great opportunity, we should rejoice, appreciate it, and feel that we are greatly fortunate. Inspired by bodhichitta, we should do our best to take full advantage of this opportunity by contemplating the Buddha's precious teachings as much as we can.

The Buddha's Vast Bodhichitta

The Buddha had inconceivable wisdom and infinite skill that he used to benefit others. One such exemplary story is that of Kisa Gotami, a distraught mother who went on to become an elder nun under the Buddha's guidance:

There was once a mother whose baby died soon after being born. She loved the baby so much that she could not accept his death and felt that there must be some way to bring the baby back to life. In desperation, she went to many different teachers to request them to revive her child. She went from place to place without food or sleep, but no one could help her. Finally, she met the Buddha and begged, "Please help me restore my child's life. You must do something or I will die, too." Seeing her tremendous agony, the Buddha was overwhelmed with compassion and considered how he might help her.

Instead of telling the mother that there was nothing that could be done, the Buddha skillfully asked her to leave the baby's body with him and go around in that village to gather a handful of mustard seed from a house where no one had ever died. If she could do that, the Buddha told her, he could do something to bring her child back. The mother was thrilled, and she ran from house to house asking whether anyone there had ever died and, if not, for a handful of mustard seed. At home after home, the residents told her how their family member had died and how much they were missed. Some of the deceased were old, some were young, and she soon realized that everyone feels the same agony and mental suffering when a loved one dies. In the end, she felt relief, because she understood that her baby's death was not unique, that everyone dies. She realized that she had no choice but to accept it. The heaviness in her heart lifted.

The mother went back to the Buddha and told him that she had not found any mustard seeds, and asked what she should do now. The Buddha said, "You see, this is the reality of impermanence. All of us who are born will die one day. We have no choice other than to accept it. We can only try to overcome this suffering by releasing our attachment and grasping. This doesn't mean that we don't care about others or give up our love. We support and help others when they are in need. That way, we can live peacefully by keeping our mind free of pain and suffering." From then on, she faithfully followed the Buddha's teachings.

Thus, we can see that the Buddha helps all sentient beings without judgment or prejudice because of the perfection of his bodhichitta. Inspired by this story, we should fully embrace bodhichitta in our heart and try diligently to apply it to our daily life. Having done that, we can die with a clear mind that is full of love and compassion.

Cultivating and Applying Bodhichitta

We try to survive by doing whatever we can, according to our interests. Whether we spend our days in business, politics, Dharma study, farming, driving a taxi, or science, we do all these things to bring some happiness into our life, because we want to free ourselves from suffering. That is our universal goal. Since bodhichitta has the same goal, we can apply it to every aspect of our lives.

Within samsara, there is physical suffering and mental suffering, and also physical happiness and mental happiness. Now, think carefully: Is physical happiness and comfort more important, or is mental peace and happiness more important? Is physical suffering stronger than mental suffering? All of our technology can indeed provide comfort and benefit to many people. It can free us from many kinds of physical suffering, but it cannot relieve our mental suffering. No matter how much we have materially, it cannot give us real mental comfort and satisfaction. Even if someone owned the whole planet, it would still not be enough. We could own the moon, Mars, and all the other planets, even other galaxies, but we would still desire more. What, then, is the purpose of all this samsaric involvement? If we were to apply even a small part of bodhichitta, we would enjoy pure peace in this life and the next.

The purpose of life is to have peace and to be free from the suffering of feeling dissatisfied and malcontent. We need some material things for physical comfort, but we must recognize that such comfort is temporary, changing every moment. On the other hand, finding mental comfort through wisdom can bring enlightenment. That was what the Buddha taught—a universal method to see precisely the respective causes of suffering and happiness. Look at the mind full of negative thoughts and afflicting emotions, and compare it to a peaceful mind full of wisdom and happiness. Look carefully. Do not look outside of yourself at what someone else is doing, but rather look into your own mind. Ask yourself, "What am I thinking? What am I doing?" Then utilize the Buddha's teaching to minimize the causes of mental suffering and to cultivate positive thoughts. Cultivating wisdom and compassion is the cause of true peace and happiness with which we can fulfill the purpose of our lives. We are so fortunate to have Dharma in our lives. No matter who you are, you can appreciate this and rejoice in it. We must make every effort to enrich and develop our wisdom and compassion, because bodhichitta teaches us how to become better people with an unbiased and universal mind.

In these modern times, the Buddha's teachings go hand in hand with modern science. In science, researchers investigate in the laboratory to prove their ideas and theories. Likewise, in Buddhism, everyone has the opportunity to thoroughly investigate the Dharma before following the path. Buddhism, however, goes a step further than science because it is able to deal with questions about the mind and mental states. Scientists have difficulty investigating the limitless nature of the mind because they have to depend on machines and other equipment to gather data. Their labs and telescopes are limited, whereas the "mental lab" has no such limitation. Their laboratories and great machines are useless for investigating the mind, because consciousness is not matter. We have to use the mental laboratory of study, contemplation, and meditation to understand how our mind functions. Questions about the mind can only be investigated by the mind, using wisdom, empirical reasoning, and skillful methods.

Buddhism is a modern religion in the sense that it provides methods based on wisdom and analysis. The philosophy of Buddhism can be argued logically, but at the same time, we can only actually prove it by living it, experiencing it, and engaging its meditations. We all desire peace and happiness, but this cannot be achieved by chanting a few mantras, sitting on a high throne, collecting a great deal of money, or constructing giant stupas and temples. Such things are means to support our study and practice but not ends in themselves. Peace and happiness are achieved through understanding the wisdom of the Buddha and putting it into practice. To practice is to purify our mental afflictions as much as possible. The more we purify them, the more peace, joy, and happiness we experience, because joy and happiness are the flavors of peace. Peace is not created by words or laws, but comes from a meditative state that purifies our mental afflictions and delusions. Bodhichitta allows us to purify all obscurations without exception, just as the Buddha did, and to accomplish all the excellent qualities of enlightenment.

Afflictions and delusions cannot be uprooted by taking a pill or wearing nice clothes. No matter how many pills you take or beautiful clothes you buy, such things will not help you become younger; thinking so is delusion. We are deluded in samsara, and with our deluded mind we create more and more delusion—and the only flavor is suffering, one layer of it upon another, layer after layer. The Dharma gives us precise wisdom, a clear mind. It shows us what is called the mode of abiding, the way things truly are—not only for Buddhists who believe in this. This is how all phenomena function.

All of samsara and nirvana function within the laws of causality. First, we study and practice the Dharma as individuals to bring happiness and peace to our own minds. Once we gain some experience, we can share it with everyone else and start to really benefit other sentient beings. Merely performing perfunctory rituals is not enough. Rituals are fine, but to perform them properly, we must have the goal of buddhahood in mind and a foundation of clear understanding. Then performing rituals, chanting mantras, reciting prayers, and so forth can reinforce what we know, and they become truly precious methods to enhance mental clarity.

The mind is unimaginably complicated and can only be comprehended through relative and absolute bodhichitta.

To encompass that complexity of the mind, the Buddha gave complete teachings not just once or using just one method. The Dharma encompasses methods to dispel *all* delusions and obscurations. The Buddha's teachings were not given to benefit just a few followers, or even just for Buddhists, but rather for every sentient being. That is why we pray, "May all mother sentient beings have happiness, and may they be free from suffering." We do not pray, "May all *Buddhists* be happy and successful." We pray for the welfare of every sentient being, including animals, fish, spirits, small bugs, and so forth. That is the Buddha's teaching. His mind extended universally, able to perceive every sentient being's feelings. No one was left outside the Buddha's umbrella of compassion.

We pray for all mother sentient beings because we all equally desire peace and happiness and also desire to be free from suffering. No one appreciates suffering and undesirable conditions. This has been true since beginningless time. For billions and trillions of eons we have stayed in samsara, life after life. As we have repeatedly cycled through the various realms over that vast period of time, every sentient being has been our mother in one or another lifetime. This is not necessarily restricted just to lives as human beings, but includes lives as animals, insects, spirits, and so on. In every case, mothers sacrifice for their children. It is from that point of view that we consider all sentient beings as our mothers.

All beings are considered to be equal because they all equally want peace and happiness. There is not a particle of difference. We all desire to be free from suffering. No matter what superficial differences we can find in our belief systems, cultures, or languages, in reality we want the same thing. So, from that point of view, we are all equal.

We make artificial distinctions because of our dualistic thoughts, which are rooted in great ignorance. Based on ignorance, confusion arises; within that confusion, we create duality. Because of our perception of dualities, we make distinctions such as *us* and *them*. First, we mistakenly think of "I" as if it were an independently existent entity, then "my"—my body, my family, my property—follows close behind. Then comes the perception of the other, *them*. So, between *us* and *them*, we protect what is ours and oppose those who create obstacles for our wishes and desires. Hatred and anger arise and the errors continue to multiply. We forget about altruism and are entangled in conflict. Regardless of who we are in terms of ideology, culture, or belief, we are all in that vicious cycle of suffering and the causes of suffering. No matter how successful your life is or how famous you are, it's like honey on a razor's edge. Dharma, especially the practice of bodhichitta, is the only solution for confusion. When we finally realize the universal nature of emptiness, we'll see that there is no difference between my innate nature and anyone else's, whether they are my enemy or a buddha. That realization ends our work to solve the puzzle of samsara.

Bodhichitta and the Buddha's Parinirvana

After teaching for forty-five years, the Buddha showed the whole world that everyone must die—even an enlightened being. The Buddha announced to his disciples that he would die in Kushinagar and there enter parinirvana. The Buddha achieved the vajra body, absolute dharmakaya, to show us how to live our lives with wisdom and how to live in a positive way, performing good deeds, so that when we die, we die with dignity and joy, and without fear. Reflect on that. The Buddha gave these teachings more than 2,600 years ago, and they are still fresh because they are not related to culture or belief. Cultures change, but the Dharma doesn't need to be updated. It is universal law. The mental afflictions that are experienced in samsara—ignorance, attachment, aversion, anger, greed, and so on—will never change; they will never cause peace and happiness. They are the same afflictions that people experienced in ancient times. Likewise, love, compassion, bodhichitta, serenity, and clarity of mind—the causes of happiness—will always be fresh and relevant. If you want peace and happiness, there is no choice but to follow the Dharma. There is no excuse, no negotiating, and no second option. No matter who we are, we need the Dharma teachings.

When Buddha Shakyamuni entered parinirvana in Kushinagar, he dissolved into dharmakaya, the absolute state of all buddhas. Dissolving into dharmakaya means that all obscurations have completely dissolved into emptiness; not even the subtle imprint of an obscuration is left. All concepts, including "self" and "nonself," all the imprints of form and the afflicted skandhas, even the most subtle mental skandhas, are fully purified within the framework of dharmakaya. In that state there is absolute joy—with all the defilements purified, all that remains is wisdom, the unafflicted dharmakaya, which has the nature of total joy. The state of dharmakaya is also free from the duality of samsara and nirvana, because all duality has been completely transcended. Since its nature cannot change, it is said to be permanent. This does not mean that it is something substantial or material, but rather that the quality, the reality, of that nature never changes.

Many scholars believe that the Buddha ceased to exist following his parinirvana, and never again incarnated, but that is not the case. The Buddha still benefits sentient beings and will continue to do so as long as space remains because of his bodhichitta. Despite the conventional appearance of having entered parinirvana in front of witnesses, in reality, the Buddha's manifestations and emanations will never cease to exist. The Buddha will continue to benefit sentient beings until the end of samsara. Many of our great teachers have personally seen visions of Buddha Shakyamuni, as well as other buddhas. For example, Gampopa had a vision of Buddha Shakyamuni teaching surrounded by a thousand buddhas. Whether we have such a profound connection to the Buddha depends on how much effort we exert. While we are learning about and reflecting on these holy places, we should remind ourselves to generate strong devotion. Visualize the Buddha and make a connection to him in your mind. This can be accomplished by developing bodhichitta. Bodhichitta is the ultimate method to unite your mind with that of the Buddha.

To cultivate bodhichitta, the cause of freedom from samsara, we first have to look at the suffering of samsara. We have already talked about the three types of suffering: the suffering of suffering, the suffering of change, and pervasive or conditioned suffering. When you look at the suffering of all sentient beings, you will be overwhelmed. You may say, "I do not want to look at that. It is too much for me." However, reflecting on this suffering has many benefits. When we first see that all suffering—regardless of who is suffering—is based on causes, it gives us the courage to face suffering. Without a cause, no result will manifest. This understanding becomes a method for cultivating compassion and wisdom.

Contemplate this way: "I want to become free from suffering, not just from my obvious suffering now, but also from any future suffering. As I fear that maybe tomorrow I will get sick or have some other problem, I seek freedom from all suffering now. Similarly, every sentient being has the same feeling I do, whether they are sophisticated or not, whether they are more prepared or not. Everyone, even a small insect, wants to be free from suffering." Reflect on this, and you will develop compassion. Without a good understanding of suffering, there is no basis for developing compassion. When we have a good understanding of the suffering of all sentient beings, we have a compelling reason to cultivate compassion and progress toward enlightenment.

As you can see, wisdom helps us to develop compassion, and compassion helps us to develop wisdom. We need wisdom to identify the cause of suffering. Otherwise, compassion is just emotional and limited to the few people we love. When we are sick, we try to find the best doctor to give us the best medicine and advice on how to improve our condition. Similarly, when we suffer, we should desperately look for the wisdom and solutions that will free us from that suffering. Although everyone is trying their best to free themselves from suffering, many of them make mistakes. They do not know the causes of suffering, and so they end up creating more suffering for themselves. When, based on our wisdom and understanding, we see that happening, we should develop greater compassion—not just for our own friends and relatives, but for every sentient being, regardless of who they are. By realizing how samsaric suffering is caused by afflicting emotions and negative actions, we enhance our wisdom and understanding of the law of causality, which is the nature of samsara.

On the path of practicing bodhichitta, we have to utilize all good feelings, relationships, and conditions, as well as bad feelings, relationships, and conditions. For example, when you encounter someone who is angry with you, realize that that person is indeed suffering. If he were not suffering, he would not have done anything hurtful. Someone who is compassionate and has a relaxed mind will not create problems. It is someone who is angry and upset that creates suffering, problems, and obstacles. When that happens, you just need to relax and reflect within yourself. Think about bodhichitta first, and develop compassion for that person. Then wish for that harmful person, as well as all other sentient beings, to avoid making negative karma, to be free from suffering, and to develop bodhichitta. Whether you can change that person or not, at least this will help give you a sense of serenity and peace. Unless your mind is peaceful and clear, you have no resources with which to help others. You are practicing bodhichitta and developing the strength of your own mind, so it will not be defeated by obstacles and suffering. Instead, your mind will grow full of courage, wisdom, and compassion. Having bodhichitta does not mean just being nice. Rather, it is strength and courage based on wisdom and compassion. So, utilize all the positive and negative conditions you encounter. Transform them into your path toward enlightenment. In this way, it is possible to transform samsara into nirvana and then you can connect with all the sentient beings.

The Buddha fully realized the nature of reality. He never said that he invented his philosophy of interdependent origination to achieve enlightenment. Rather, he uncovered the truth that interdependence is simply the nature of reality. Interdependent origination means that everything functions within the law of karma, and that nothing can function outside the bounds of causes and conditions. All the Buddha's teachings are based on the wisdom of that understanding. To see that for yourself, start by looking at the suffering of all sentient beings, then look to see whether there is any way to end that suffering. Perhaps taking a magic pill? Maybe buying a new car? Traveling to the moon or another galaxy? No, the only thing we can do is clean up ourselves. We do that by generating and cultivating our own wisdom, compassion, and bodhichitta. The solution is to achieve buddhahood; this is the absolute solution to suffering. This is why we have to cultivate bodhichitta.

The following prayer is a familiar support for our development of bodhichitta:

> Bodhichitta, the excellent and precious mind:
> where it is unborn, may it arise;
> where it is born, may it not decline,
> but ever increase higher and higher.

We may close our eyes and look sincere while chanting this verse, but do we really know what it means? We should let it become deeply embedded in our heart. When we feel good, we chant this prayer, but when we feel bad, our mind goes somewhere else. We should endeavor to change that, and let this prayer guide us no matter what our inner or outer circumstances may be.

Bodhichitta is a Sanskrit word; in Tibetan, it is *jangchup sempa*. *Jang* means "to purify all the mental obscurations"; *chup* means "to achieve," in this case to achieve perfect wisdom. Together, they mean "using wisdom to purify the obscurations."

Jangchup and *sempa* together mean that we develop the mind (*sem*) through compassion and wisdom. Having compassion is very important, but by itself it is not enough to make one a buddha. Some people naturally have very strong compassion. When they see suffering, their compassion is so strong that tears build up in their eyes. But without wisdom, there is no solution to that suffering. On the other hand, there are some people who naturally have great wisdom. Intellectually, they know everything well and can explain complex ideas with precision, but they lack compassion. To cultivate bodhichitta, both compassion and wisdom are indispensable. If either is missing, bodhichitta cannot arise. It is necessary to build our courage, based on wisdom, to uproot delusions. That is what bodhichitta practice is about. We don't cultivate bodhichitta to appear nice and smiling. Just wearing robes, for example, does not increase one's bodhichitta. Clothes do not eliminate mental afflictions. Wearing robes can support one's practice, but besides that, there is not much benefit to it if internally your afflicting emotions are in control.

In Tibet, there is a widely known story that demonstrates the transformative power of bodhichitta:

There is well-known mountain pass where people passed back and forth every day. Around the eleventh or twelfth century, a notorious robber operated there and attacked those who traveled over the pass. If someone tried to ignore him, he beat them until he had knocked them down. It was known that it was unwise to cross there except with a large group of people. One time, an old woman had some urgent business and was forced to cross the mountain pass alone. As she walked, she was constantly worried that the robber might show up any minute. Near the top, a stranger approached her, and she thought that he would be a good companion to protect her from danger. So they walked and chatted together all the way to the top of the mountain. While they took a rest, she took a long breath and told him, "I'm happy we arrived here on top of this pass. I feel so comfortable with you here." Then she asked him, "By the way, there is supposed to be a robber around here named Ben Kungyal. Have you ever seen him or met him?" To her surprise he replied, "That is me." She was so completely shocked that she died right there in front of him.

The robber himself was shocked and thought, "What kind of terrible person am I, that just by hearing my name, people literally fall dead in front of me? This is not the right way to live. I must change my life." He considered what to do, and he had the idea to study and practice the Dharma. He started meeting teachers from the Kadampa school and receiving Dharma teachings. His bad habit of stealing from others continued for a while, but he also continued to practice purifying his deeply rooted negative habits. He went into retreat for months, and then for years, coming out to receive teachings and then going back into retreat. People slowly began to trust him and to think of him as a sincere practitioner. In the end, he stayed in a cave and devoted the rest of his life to meditation. The local people started going to see him to receive blessings, request teachings, and make offerings. By the end of his life, his cave was full of offerings from the villagers. He said,

"The power of the Dharma and the practice of bodhichitta, what great magic! When I was a young, strong
robber, I barely had enough to eat. Now that I am in solitary retreat, offerings are pouring into my cave. Bodhichitta truly is the cause of peace and happiness!"

The Dharma can change our lives, too, if we take it to heart. If
we practice to sincerely purify our mental afflictions and delusions, without doubt, the result will be obvious. Take some
time to look at your own mind seriously. There is no shortcut,
no magic. Every day we must bring the Dharma into our mind
and, especially, remind ourselves of bodhichitta: "May I be
useful to all sentient beings. May my body, speech, and mind
be a source of peace and wisdom for others." We must meditate on this and purify all our limitations, shortcomings, and
mental afflictions. We must practice like this to bring out our
good qualities as much as possible.

Even if we do not have any expectations of results, great
peace and harmony will be present within the mind wherever
we are. Suppose we eat a very simple lunch. It may not be very
good, but we can still appreciate it and rejoice: "I am so happy
because I have a precious human life and I can practice the
Dharma. I am especially fortunate to have connected with the
profound Vajrayana teachings." Rejoice and continue to practice. The Dharma is more than a collection of interesting bits
of knowledge. The Dharma explains universal causality—the
wisdom of what is right and what is wrong—which brings us
peace and happiness.

The Bodhichitta Ceremony

Perhaps this discussion has inspired you to develop bodhichitta yourself. Consider whether you have developed compassion for all beings, whether you recognize the ubiquitous nature of suffering and find it intolerable, and whether you aspire to become enlightened so that you can help all beings become free of the ravages of samsara. If so, try to seek out a spiritual master to conduct the bodhisattva vow ceremony. If that is not possible, you can take the bodhisattva vow on your own by performing the ceremony by yourself according to the following guide:

> Visualize Buddha Shakyamuni, the embodiment of wisdom and compassion, surrounded by the buddhas of the past, present, and future in the space in front of you. They are surrounded by Dharma texts, bodhisattvas, and all the great Dharma teachers you know. The entirety of space is filled with buddhas, bodhisattvas, masters, and texts. In front of all these buddhas and bodhisattvas, take refuge in the Buddha, in the Dharma teachings of all three vehicles, and in the Sangha, all the great bodhisattvas, until you achieve buddhahood. Keep in mind that you do this for the benefit of all sentient beings, and recite three times:

> > Until I attain enlightenment, I take refuge in all
> > the buddhas,
> > I take refuge in the Dharma, and likewise in the
> > Sangha.

In this case, taking refuge includes keeping the five precepts—not killing, not stealing, not lying, not taking intoxicants, and not engaging in sexual misconduct. These disciplines are the foundation for cultivating bodhichitta and, especially, for maintaining the practice of bodhichitta.

To cultivate bodhichitta, take all the buddhas of the past as your examples. They saw the nature of samsara and the suffering of all sentient beings, and they cultivated bodhichitta. Afterward, they practiced bodhichitta, and through the three trainings—training in moral conduct, training in meditative absorption, and training in wisdom awareness—they purified all their obscurations and became buddhas. In front of all those buddhas, first cultivate aspiration bodhichitta and then resolve to put it into action by practicing the six perfections, or paramitas: generosity, moral ethics, patience, perseverance, meditative concentration, and wisdom awareness. These six perfections are the means to purify mental obscurations and become a buddha. Again keeping in mind that you do this for the benefit of all sentient beings, recite three times:

> As the previous buddhas embraced the enlightened mind
> and progressed on the bodhisattva path,
> I, too, for the benefit of all sentient beings,
> give birth to bodhichitta
> and apply myself to accomplishing the stages of the path.

Meditate that you have fully cultivated bodhichitta, while the visualized buddhas, Dharma, and Sangha dissolve into light. That light dissolves into the crown of your head and flows down to pervade your body, speech, and mind. Meditate that your mind and the Buddha's mind become inseparable. Meditate in the natural mahamudra state of emptiness, which is ultimate bodhichitta. Your mind becomes free of all contrived fabrications.

This is the beginning of the Dharma journey toward enlightenment. As the Buddha practiced the Dharma, and especially bodhichitta, for three limitless *kalpas*, today you, too, are developing mental strength and courage. Cultivate a commitment to bodhichitta by thinking, "No matter what happens, even at the risk of my life, I will never give up bodhichitta. I will follow this path and purify all my mental obscurations. I will attain buddhahood to benefit all sentient beings. I have no choice but to do this."

To end, rejoice in your accomplishment by thinking, "Today, my life became meaningful. This precious human life has brought a great result—because of it, I have an opportunity to cultivate and practice bodhichitta, which means I follow the path of the bodhisattvas." Then declare to others, "Be happy, all you sentient beings, I am here for you." Rejoice in having cultivated bodhichitta, the precious and most holy mind that is the direct cause of buddhahood. This is the true way to end suffering.

We can chant the bodhichitta verse from the ceremony above at any time. And as we take refuge in the Buddha, Dharma, and Sangha, we should see them as special objects for our own peace and happiness. We should also feel concern for all other sentient beings after seeing how confused they are. Our goal is to develop impartial love and compassion toward them all without reservation. Even so, sometimes we create the causes of more suffering. Using the eye of wisdom and bodhichitta, be aware of this, and develop a strong sense of remorse. Regret that bewilderment and mental delusions have pushed you to create suffering for yourself and others. Then reinforce your practice of bodhichitta so that everyone on the planet may experience harmony and serenity.

The most important aspect of training in aspiration bodhichitta is never forsaking any sentient being, not even your bitterest enemies. You must keep them in your mind, wishing that they be free from suffering, have peace and happiness while in samsara, and eventually achieve complete enlightenment.

Training in Action Bodhichitta: The Six Perfections in Thirteen Topics

To train in action bodhichitta, we practice the six perfections, or paramitas. These are methods for purifying our physical, verbal, and mental obscurations which are the root cause of undesirable suffering. These six are ways to unite our mind with the Buddha's mind—or in other words, to reveal our unfabricated and uncontrived nature. If we practice them without bodhichitta, they can be a path to becoming a shravaka or pratyekabuddha. If we practice them with bodhichitta, they become the path to buddhahood.

There are many books about the practice of the six perfections. You can read about them in detail in Gampopa's *Jewel Ornament of Liberation*, Shantideva's *Engaging in the Bodhisattva's Way of Life*, and others to support your practice. Here, I will describe the six perfections with thirteen topics that explain their main points. This presentation derives from a commentary on Jigten Sumgön's classic *One Thought*, or *Gongchik*.

1. Overview

The practice of the first three perfections—generosity, moral ethics, and patience—cause one to achieve the two bodies of a buddha, the sambhogakaya and nirmanakaya. The last two—meditative concentration and wisdom awareness—are the cause for achievement of the dharmakaya. Perseverance is the cause to perfect all three.

2. Functions

The practice of generosity eliminates the condition of poverty. The practice of moral ethics helps us achieve coolness, freeing us from the heat of the mental afflictions, and subsequently the suffering of the lower realms. Forbearance eliminates anger and resentment. Perseverance joins its practitioner with the supreme achievement of enlightenment. Meditative concentration protects us from having a scattered mind. Wisdom lets us realize the ultimate meaning. Of these, Nagarjuna said,

> Generosity and discipline, patience, diligence,
> concentration, and the wisdom that knows thusness—
> those measureless perfections, make them grow,
> and be a Mighty Conqueror who's crossed samsara's sea.[7]

The six perfections are like a bow or boat, with the practitioner being an arrow shot by the bow or a merchant riding in the boat. Nirvana is the target of the arrow and the destination of the boat.

3. Characteristics

The perfection of each of the six perfections of the bodhisattvas is categorized into four characteristics: they decrease their opposite; they produce the primordial wisdom of nonconceptual thought; they fulfill all that is desired; and they mature sentient beings in the ways of the shravaka, pratyekabuddha, and bodhisattva. Regarding the first set of characteristics, generosity dispels stinginess, moral ethics dispels immorality, patience dispels anger, perseverance dispels laziness, meditative concentration dispels heedlessness, and wisdom dispels distorted intelligence. The other three characteristics are the same for all six perfections.

Practicing these six purifies the causes of suffering that oppose each of the perfections. By thus purifying our mental delusions, we support the nonconceptual realization of wisdom. By perfecting these six, we gradually progress toward buddhahood. Once a practitioner is well equipped and skilled in these practices, he or she has the ability to benefit other sentient beings according to their capacity.

4. Divisions

Each practice of the six perfections has three divisions:

(1) The practice of generosity: giving material objects, giving Dharma teachings, and giving protection from fear.

(2) The practice of morality: refraining from nonvirtuous

thoughts and actions, performing virtuous deeds, and benefitting sentient beings.

(3) The practice of patience: not being concerned about harm from others, accepting suffering without fear, and practicing the profound and vast Dharma with certainty.

(4) The practice of perseverance: application (applying Dharma study and practice consistently), armor (always being ready to practice in order to attain complete enlightenment), and insatiability (never stopping one's study and practice until one becomes a buddha).

(5) The practice of meditative concentration: one-pointed concentration in the desire world, form world, and formless world (see appendix C); focusing the one-pointed mind on suchness, or the nonreferential nature of mind; and concentration on the virtuous practice of the unafflicted nature.

(6) The practice of wisdom awareness: study; contemplation; and meditation on the absolute, on understanding the inseparable nature of the relative and ultimate states.

Thus, by considering that each of the six perfections has three divisions, we have eighteen perfections to practice. Each of the eighteen should in turn be practiced by keeping six goals in mind: (1) benefitting sentient beings, (2) not harming sentient beings, (3) forbearing with sickness and suffering, (4) practicing without being interrupted by other activities, (5) practicing without distraction, and (6) practicing all this within the framework of emptiness. By thus practicing the eighteen perfections in each of these six ways, we have in total 108 perfection practices.

5. Groupings

Great masters have grouped the perfections in various ways. According to Maitreya's *Ornament of the Mahayana Sutras* (*Mahayanasutralamkara*), generosity and moral ethics are grouped as the accumulation of merit, wisdom is the accumulation of wisdom awareness, and the other three—patience, perseverance, and meditative concentration—belong to both accumulations. However, if they are sealed by the wisdom of emptiness, all six can be counted as the accumulation of wisdom. In Chandrakirti's *Supplement to the Middle Way* (*Madhyamakavatara*), the practices of generosity, moral ethics, and patience comprise the accumulation of merit; meditative concentration and wisdom awareness are grouped as the accumulation of wisdom; and perseverance belongs to both categories. Atisha, the great eleventh-century Indian master who helped revive Buddhism in Tibet, said that the first five comprise the accumulation of merit, and wisdom awareness alone supports the accumulation of wisdom.

6. Superior aspects

There are two superior aspects to the practice of the six perfections: superior motivation while practicing the six perfections and superior objects of one's practice. With the following superior motivations, the six perfections become a superior means to attain buddhahood.

- There is greater merit in practicing generosity without expectation of a favorable return.
- There is greater merit in practicing moral ethics without expectation of a better rebirth.
- There is greater merit in practicing patience that is done equally toward all.

- There is greater merit in practicing perseverance that distinguishes between faults and good qualities.
- There is greater merit in practicing meditation while not attached to achieving the form or formless realm.
- There is greater merit in practicing wisdom that is imbued with method.

The following superior objects of practice provide the skillful means that channel your practice toward buddhahood without getting sidetracked.

- Giving the wisdom of the Dharma is the superior object of generosity.
- Moral ethics practiced with the realization of wisdom is the superior practice that delights the buddhas.
- Patience practiced within the context of understanding the unborn meaning of emptiness is the superior practice.
- Perseverance practiced within the context of the Mahayana is superior.
- Meditative concentration that abandons the four extremes—existence, nonexistence, neither existence nor nonexistence, and both existence and nonexistence—is superior.
- Wisdom practice endowed with compassion is superior.

7. Things to be abandoned

There are two categories of things to be abandoned: inferior ways to practice and attitudes that cause your practice to deteriorate. Abandon these inferior ways to practice:

- Practicing generosity that is just a display to attract others for business or self-aggrandizement

- Practicing fabricated moral ethics that pretend to be pure discipline
- Practicing patience for show, with peaceful speech and body but not mind
- Practicing perseverance temporarily while others are watching
- Practicing meditative concentration that isolates body and speech but not mind
- Practicing wisdom that merely shows skill in talking and repetition

Abandon these factors that cause your practice to deteriorate:
- Practicing generosity while still attached to wealth
- Practicing moral ethics that ignore minor or subtle matters
- Practicing patience with pride
- Practicing perseverance while attached to merit
- Practicing meditation in order to enjoy the pleasant feeling
- Practicing wisdom with scattered thoughts

As Dharma practitioners, we must pay attention to these topics so that all the practices we do will be productive and not waste our time and energy. If done properly in a superior way, even a small amount of practice can bring great benefit.

8. Purposes
Each of the six perfections has four purposes, making twenty-four in all. Their purposes are:

(1) To free us from rebirth in the lower realms

(2) To cause us to enjoy the happiness of humans and gods, even if we don't expect it

(3) To cause us to continuously enjoy precious Dharma practice

(4) To purify all our gross and subtle obscurations, which leads us to complete buddhahood and, ultimately, to the benefit of all sentient beings

9. Results

Practice of the six perfections has four results:

(1) The result of karmic ripening is the attainment of the dharmakaya, sambhogakaya, and nirmanakaya, as well as their respective activities.

(2) There are two types of results that accord with the cause: in terms of one's activity and in terms of one's experience. In terms of activity, one naturally wants to give without reservation until one reaches buddhahood; one always tends toward the practice of generosity; and one finds it difficult to turn away from generosity. These should be applied similarly to the rest of the perfections.

In terms of experience, the result of generosity is an abundance of wealth and enjoyments; the result of moral ethics is that one attains a superior rebirth; the result of patience is an excellent body; the result of perseverance is a continuous increase in virtuous qualities; the result of meditative concentration is attainment of the six types of clairvoyance; and the result of wisdom is to remove mental afflictions from their root.

(3) The environmental result is that one will be born in a sacred place where the Dharma is practiced. Practicing the six perfections is also a direct way to take care of the environment.

The disasters we are currently facing are the result of our collective failure to practice the ten virtues and the six perfections.

(4) The separation from negative actions that results from practice frees us from the factors that oppose the six perfections: stinginess; distorted morality; anger; laziness, especially with regard to Dharma practice; distractions; and distorted wisdom. These results are not only good for one's Dharma practice, but good for the entire world. Linking oneself to these negative factors will cause unfavorable conditions for anyone, not just Buddhists.

10. Categories

The six perfections can be categorized according to the three higher trainings: morality, meditation, and wisdom.

- The practices of generosity, moral ethics, and patience are included within the superior training in morality. Through generosity, a discipline free from grasping arises. The practice of patience enables one to maintain discipline. When we practice moral ethics, we may encounter a lot of obstacles; patience gives us strength to face them positively.
- The practice of perseverance supports all three higher trainings.
- The practice of meditative concentration is the higher training in meditation.
- The practice of wisdom awareness is the higher training in wisdom.

Engaging in the three higher trainings is like taking the highway toward buddhahood. All Buddhist schools throughout the world have a high regard for them. In terms of the higher trainings, moral ethics means avoiding all the causes of suffering within the context of the monastic Vinaya code, bodhisattva training, and Vajrayana practice alike. Virtuous practices are the foundation of the Buddha's teachings. Once one is fully trained in moral ethics, one has the ability to work with the mind, to stabilize it and establish clarity. It is very difficult to stabilize the mind without the support of moral ethics. Thus, through moral ethics one is well prepared for good meditative concentration, the second higher training. When the mind is quiet and experiences equipoise in the state of calm abiding, then the third training, wisdom, is well endowed. A clear mind allows the light of special insight to be aroused without much difficulty. This is the great opportunity to uproot all the mental afflictions that cause us to wander in samsara. Because their nature is empty, we have the ability to achieve the realization that we have been buddhas right from the beginning. The Buddha summed up his teachings this way in the *Dhammapada*:

> Abandon evil.
> Accomplish virtue.
> Thus train your mind.
> This is the teaching of all the buddhas.

11. Sequences

The sequencing of the six perfections is explained in three ways: the order in which they arise in the mind, from lower to higher, and from coarse to subtle.

The first sequence is the order in which they arise in the mind. Once you have developed the practice of generosity, the thought arises, "What more can I do?" Moral ethics then arises in a natural and genuine way. Without grasping to hinder you, you feel so happy to accept the virtues that are to be accomplished and the nonvirtues that are to be purified. Moral ethics leads you easily to the practice of patience. With negativity pacified and the causes of peace, happiness, and harmony gathered, your mind is well prepared to be patient. Once you enjoy patience, you can make effort in your Dharma practice with perseverance. Through persevering in these practices, your unruly mind has been made gentle, and a gentle mind is conducive to calm abiding and meditative concentration. With your mind thus well equipped with good qualities, you can achieve the state of samadhi. This provides the clarity and mental strength to counteract all the negative forces of the mind. When you abide in meditation, you will be able to see reality as it is. That is wisdom—the clear, incisive mind that understands the true nature of reality.

The second sequence is from lower to higher. The lower practices are listed first, leading gradually up to the higher ones. Thus, moral ethics is superior to generosity; patience is superior to moral ethics because it is more difficult and more profound; and so on, until you reach wisdom awareness, which is the highest and most important. However, this is not to say that the "lower" perfections are somehow not important. You have to depend on the first five as a method to attain wisdom, but without wisdom you cannot be freed from samsara. Wisdom alone gives you the opportunity to realize the emptiness of all phenomena.

The third sequence is from coarse to subtle. Practices that are easier to follow are listed first and those that are subtle and difficult to follow are explained later. For example, giving a small amount of food or money away is easy. Keeping one's precepts and abiding by the ten virtues is harder. Some people are quite diligent, but cannot meditate for a minute. The first five perfections are all easier than achieving the realization of emptiness.

This topic of sequencing allows us to understand how the six perfections are connected to each other. Many try to jump into subtle subjects, such as mahamudra, without paying attention to the coarser practices, like generosity and moral ethics. As a practical matter, they are not well prepared, and the expected results will not materialize despite their enthusiasm. We must all go step by step through the practices. It takes time, just as a tree takes many years to bear its first fruit. To gain benefit from our practices, we have to carefully reflect on our own mind. If we are not really prepared, our time and energy might be wasted. Of course, all Dharma practice has benefit, but if we act prematurely we will not achieve our desired results, because the proper causes and conditions are missing.

12. Accomplishment of a higher rebirth and liberation
One accomplishes a higher rebirth and liberation from samsara through the practice of the six perfections. The first four perfections lead to higher rebirth and enjoyments in the following ways:

- Generosity of material possessions is the direct cause of abundant wealth. Giving fearlessness to those who are in danger brings peace and happiness to your life. Giving wisdom to those who lack skill frees you from having a lack of intelligence in future lives.
- By abstaining from nonvirtuous deeds and performing virtuous deeds, you gain a perfect body—that is, a precious human life.

- The practice of patience purifies all the mental afflictions, but particularly anger and resentment. When in this way your mind becomes more peaceful, peace prevails in your life and in society as a whole. As a result, people like you, and you can gather an excellent retinue. You will enjoy peace and happiness in this life, and the next life will be better.
- Perseverance is the indispensable support for all these practices. With diligence, all your endeavors will be completed. Continuously progress and develop good qualities without becoming satisfied by small achievements. This is the basis for you to make a better world, for peace and happiness, and finally for freedom from suffering and the achievement of liberation.

The last two perfections lead to liberation. Meditative concentration reduces the strength of the mental afflictions, and wisdom completely uproots them.

Regarding this wisdom, it is important to note that only the wisdom of the Dharma contains the method to eliminate confusion. Every day, new inventions appear to make our lives easier, but if we are not careful, they will also bring unwanted side effects. We can become distracted by electronics, for instance. As consumers, we have to adjust to new technologies mindfully so we do not become enslaved by them and left with no time for anything else. If you really want a good life, purify your mental delusions and the bad habits that cause suffering. This has nothing to do with culture or belief systems. The Dharma is relevant to everyone's peace and happiness—in this life and the next. The real message of the Buddha is this kind of wisdom that can be studied and applied by everyone.

13. Benefits for others and oneself

The first three perfections benefit other sentient beings:

- Generosity directly benefits others.
- With moral ethics, you abandon harm to others.
- Patience prevents you from retaliating when someone harms you.

Perseverance benefits others and oneself. The last two, meditative concentration and wisdom, purify your mental afflictions and uproot all your defilements.

Keep Bodhichitta in Your Heart

As long as you have bodhichitta and the practice of the six perfections, nothing but peace and happiness will come. They are a precondition to the introduction of your inner wisdom. At the time of death, you have to leave everything else behind; you can't carry even a penny. With bodhichitta, however, you will always feel rich, happy, and satisfied. It provides everything you need for your mind, so keep this wealth in your heart. Continually remind yourself of the beneficial effects of bodhichitta. Bodhichitta is the best wealth that you can have. You can keep this kind of wealth lifetime after lifetime, until you become a buddha. All other types of samsaric wealth are limited to this one lifetime—plus, sometimes, instead of giving benefit, they become a source of suffering. You have to constantly protect yourself against that. Make every effort to train in bodhichitta. Exercise your heart by bringing love and compassion to all sentient beings. Check to see what mistakes you are making that are contrary to bodhichitta, and make an effort to avoid them. Build the bodhichitta stupa before spending time and resources on a rock and brick stupa. Build the temple of bodhichitta in your heart.

This chapter provided just a short summary of the Buddha's teachings to remind ourselves of why we follow these teachings and why we practice. We follow the Buddha's teachings because they are the method to free ourselves from suffering, the method to bring us all true peace and happiness. We don't follow the Buddha just because our friends and family do, or out of habit or cultural tradition. We follow our wisdom that realizes that the cause of suffering is universal. The same factors cause suffering for everyone—for those who know about this and those who do not know, for those who practice Dharma and those who do not. The causes for happiness are also the same for everyone, not just for Buddhists. Because of the great importance of bodhichitta, we must pay particular attention to its practice.

Maya, the queen of that god-like king,
bore in her womb the glory of her race and,
being in her purity free from weariness, sorrow and illusion,
she set her mind on the sin-free forest.

In her longing for the lonely forest as suited to trance,
she asked the king to let her go and stay in the grove called
     Lumbini,
which was gay like the garden of Caitraratha
with trees of every kind.

The lord of the earth, full of wonder and joy,
recognized that her disposition was noble from her possession
     of piety,
and let her leave the fortunate city in order to gratify her,
not for a pleasure excursion.

In that glorious grove the queen perceived
that the time of her delivery was at hand and,
amidst the welcome of thousands of waiting-women,
proceeded to a couch overspread with an awning.

Then as soon as the stars became propitious,
from the side of the queen, who was hallowed by her vows,
a son was born for the good of the world,
without her suffering either pain or illness.
—Ashvagosha, *Buddhacarita*

CHAPTER 10

Lumbini: The Fivefold Path of Mahamudra

WE KNOW without question that Lumbini is the Buddha's birthplace because a pillar erected in the third century BCE by King Ashoka, inscribed with a declaration identifying the site, was found here in 1896. The pillar has been repaired and stands in its original location. Today, the spot of the holy birth is indicated by a marker stone enclosed within the Maya Devi Temple, which was built on the ruins of a much earlier temple. The Pushkarini Pond in which Maya Devi bathed just after the birth stands nearby. Leading up to the shrine is a long central canal with Theravada structures on one side and Mahayana stupas and temples on the other. These were built by devotees from many different countries. Near the entrance are an impressive, modern peace stupa, a museum, and a research facility. UNESCO acknowledged the significance of Lumbini by declaring it to be a World Heritage Site in 1997.

For three limitless eons, the buddha-to-be accumulated virtues, purified mental obscurations, developed wisdom, and practiced to perfect bodhichitta. He consciously chose to be reborn in Lumbini to fulfill the needs of sentient beings, to show them how to achieve enlightenment. So even from the time before his miraculous delivery, the Buddha's birth was a little different from that of an ordinary being.

On the night the Buddha was conceived, Queen Maya vividly dreamed that a white elephant descended from the Tushita heaven and disappeared into her womb through her side. This was taken to be a sign that the child would be extraordinary. Later, when the time of delivery was near, the queen wanted to follow tradition and return to her family's home in Devadaha to give birth. King Shuddhodana gave his permission for this journey and provided her with every comfort and protection. She and her large entourage rested along the way at the Lumbini Grove, a beautiful park with fragrant pools and flowering trees. Unexpectedly, the time of delivery arrived while they were there. The queen did not suffer any pain whatsoever. She grasped onto a branch of a sal tree and the child emerged from her side. Divine beings caught the baby and lowered him gently to the ground, whereupon he started to walk and talk. He took seven steps in each of the cardinal directions, declaring that this was his final birth, that he was chief among humans, that he would cross the ocean of samsara, and that he would attain nirvana in this lifetime.

Queen Maya, her son, and their entourage returned to Kapilavastu, where the queen passed away a week later. The boy was named Siddhartha (He Who Accomplished His Goals) because the king was so delighted that he felt as if all his wishes had been fulfilled. Among the many well-wishers who came to see the new prince was a seer who predicted that if the child stayed in the palace, he would become a world-ruling emperor, but if he left he would become a fully enlightened buddha.

From the day he was born until he died, everything the Buddha did was done consciously to benefit sentient beings. He showed the right path, giving discourses for individuals according to their individual dispositions and capacities. The reason that so many different teachings, traditions, and lineages are taught at so many different levels is to reveal the subtlety of the mind. The infinite mind has layers upon layers of obscurations, so we have to purify it step by step. First, we purify the gross obscurations, then the subtle obscurations, and, at the end, the ultimate step is to purify the most subtle obscuration. The Buddha was born here just to teach us this.

The mind, whether it is an enlightened mind of a buddha or an unenlightened mind of a sentient being, is infinite. Like space, it has no boundary. The enlightened mind has complete awareness of everything; nothing is hidden. All the chains of causality for everything that exists in nirvana and samsara can be precisely, directly perceived as easily as seeing the palm of your hand. Thus, the Buddha was able to give teachings without missing anything. On the other hand, a sentient being's mind is obscured by adventitious defilements. These mental afflictions obscure the clarity of the mind like the sun hidden behind a cloud. We are blocked from perceiving the causes that bring peace and happiness and the causes that bring suffering. Thus, we need a powerful method to overcome our entrenched habits and obscurations; mahamudra is such a method.

The Fivefold Path of Mahamudra

The fivefold path of mahamudra is a comprehensive method by which one can attain buddhahood in a single lifetime.

It contains the entirety of the Buddha's teachings, both sutra and tantra. It is such a vital practice; as the great Jigten Sumgön said, "Mahāmudrā is like a lion: If it is not fivefold, it is eyeless."[8] Jigten Sumgön studied and practiced this five-fold path and achieved buddhahood in a single lifetime. From within the context of such wisdom and great compassion, he explained the Dharma just as the Buddha himself had taught. Without reservation, he shared this fivefold path with hundreds of thousands of disciples. Many of them attained buddhahood, and the rest achieved other stages of the bodhi-sattva's path.

The five aspects of this path are (1) the study and practice of bodhichitta, (2) *yidam* practice, (3) four-*kaya* guru yoga, (4) mahamudra, and (5) dedication. Among these practices, bodhichitta is the essence of the sutra system. Yidam deity practice is the essence of the tantra system. Guru yoga brings about the essence of the qualities of a buddha. Mahamudra illuminates the essence of the ultimate meaning. Dedication is the essence of skillful means. At the time of the Buddha, his disciple Chandraprabha Kumara fully comprehended this fivefold path. When he was reborn later in Tibet as Gampopa, it became the core of his teachings.

Bodhichitta

First, we use every skill and method to cultivate bodhichitta in our mind. Bodhichitta is the indispensable method to attain a clear, precise mind; to reveal buddha nature; and to purify all the afflictions. Long ago, all the buddhas came together and discussed the best way to eliminate the suffering of sentient beings. They concluded that the practice and perfection of bodhichitta was the supreme method to help sentient beings. The Buddha spent eons before his enlightenment perfecting the practice of bodhichitta. It is necessary for us to follow in his footsteps and cultivate bodhichitta in order to free ourselves from unwanted suffering by revealing the nature of mind. Bodhichitta is the most important essence of all the Buddha's teachings; it is the principal path, and is infused in all the Buddha's teachings. Thus, we start right from the beginning with bodhichitta, and then progress step by step until we become buddhas ourselves.

Unless we are endowed with the prerequisite practices, the so-called higher and more profound practices will not work. When the foundation is well established by the preliminaries, all our practices will be productive. It is always helpful to reflect on the foundational teachings of impermanence, suffering, and the precious human life because they are the key to buddhahood.

Regarding impermanence, we will not gain much benefit from just intellectually touching the subject. If that's all we do, it becomes a mere Buddhist belief that will not help when we need it. However, when emotional feeling and experience penetrate our heart, this approach to practicing impermanence will support our Dharma practice well. Our practice becomes alive when we really feel urgency. Then we will not waste any more time.

Next, to reflect on suffering, bring all sentient beings, yourself included, into your heart. Feel their suffering and contemplate, "I am not free from this. I am subject to the same suffering as everyone else. How can I get out of this predicament?" Recognize that the root causes of all this suffering are your mental delusions and attachment to the ego. Inventing a self that does not exist has been our common inveterate habit for a long time. So, recognize this and make an effort to develop the counteracting wisdom.

Then, to reflect on the precious human life, consider how right now, we have an inconceivably precious opportunity to access the wisdom of the Buddha. If we don't follow this wisdom and work on deconstructing our negative habits now, then when will we do it? In the other places we might be reborn, such as the animal or spirit realm, we won't have an opportunity to learn or practice the Dharma. If we are reborn there, how can we ever get out of this predicament?

To begin the cultivation of bodhichitta, we start by reflecting on the direct causes of bodhichitta: the practices of loving-kindness and compassion. Consider first how much you care for those most close to you, how much you want to help when they encounter a problem. That mind is indicative of the foundational understanding that we should gradually extend to all other sentient beings; we should see each one as if they were like our closest person. This is important to understand—all our success, even on the level of mundane achievement, is because of others. If you are in a desolate place, you cannot become famous or rich. Cherishing and respecting others is the direct cause for your success. This is causality; what you create is what you receive. Everything depends on causality. No matter whether you are a Buddhist or not, we will get the results of the causes that we create individually and collectively. Causality rules both samsara and nirvana. To see this causality directly, relative and ultimate bodhichitta are the necessary methods for overcoming ignorance and achieving enlightenment.

Based on this, cultivate loving-kindness and compassion for

all others. Practice this way not only for this life, not only for your own benefit, but with the goal of entirely freeing yourself and all others from suffering. This is the direct method of reaching out to every sentient being. By reaching out with your mind this way, you exercise the mind and purify your limitations, shortcomings, and mental delusions. Look at your mind directly to see how many negative emotions and delusions you have. They manifest constantly, without stopping. Our habituated pattern manifests unceasingly throughout our daily life, so much that it monopolizes our entire mind. We should reflect on these things and acknowledge these afflictions, which do nothing but cause suffering for ourselves and others. So purify them, each and every one, with love, compassion, and bodhichitta. Aspire to attain buddhahood in the bodhisattva's way. Once bodhichitta has been generated, use the six perfections as a special technique to accomplish enlightenment.

Yidam Practice

The second part of the fivefold path is the practice of the yidam deity, which is a method that belongs to the Vajrayana tradition. Why is Vajrayana, the tantric method, important? A buddha has two kayas: the *rupakaya*, or form body, and the dharmakaya, or wisdom body. The rupakaya consists of two forms: the nirmanakaya, or emanation body, and sambhogakaya, or enjoyment body. The nirmanakaya is a physical, material body similar to the ones we have. The sambhogakaya is an insubstantial form, a wisdom form like a rainbow, whose nature is inseparable emptiness and appearance. There is nothing to attach to, no grasping or fixation. For example, when we see the moon's reflection in a lake, we observe it but don't have any expectations about it, as we might the moon itself. Become accustomed to visualizing the yidam in this manner.

The nirmanakaya can be seen by ordinary people and great bodhisattvas; the sambhogakaya can only be seen by great bodhisattvas who are free from samsara and have achieved certain stages of the path. Following skillful instructions, in yidam practice we generate ourselves into an enlightened state in order to purify our impure mind. From within that state, all appearances manifest like a reflection or a rainbow. This gives us the opportunity to purify the mental delusions that make everything seem substantial. Bone, flesh, and blood are part of the impure perception of an afflicted mind. That is why the Vajrayana techniques and practices are so effective.

But before we engage in Vajrayana practice, we must lay a proper foundation. First, we need a strong sense of renunciation from samsara so that our Vajrayana practice becomes a cause to leave samsara, not to enrich it. To do this, contemplate the impermanence of composite phenomena. Within that context, samsara is a state of suffering; whether obvious or not, its nature is dissatisfaction. When you reflect on these topics, you gain a deep conviction that samsara has no absolute happiness or peace, and this conviction will reinforce your desire to be free of samsara. Then reflect on sentient beings with loving-kindness and compassion.

To cross the border between samsara and enlightenment, we take refuge. Taking refuge is the most important way to start our spiritual journey. It is the most important aspect of the path because all our Dharma study and practice are contained within it. Finally, we become buddhas ourselves—the embodiment of the Dharma and perfection of the Sangha.

Next, we cultivate aspiration bodhichitta on the basis of wisdom and compassion. Exercise your wisdom by reflecting on the Buddha's wisdom of knowing everything as it is. Exercise your compassion by looking at the many causes of suffering and at how beings are confused and rooted in delusion.

In order to attain buddhahood, aspirational bodhichitta is not enough. We must understand how to take action to actually accomplish buddhahood. This is the study and practice of action bodhichitta, where we follow the path of the three higher trainings or the six perfections. Within this category, one becomes well equipped in the understanding, and especially the practice, of relative bodhichitta and absolute bodhichitta. Relative bodhichitta refers to the study and practice of emptiness and the two types of selflessness. Ultimate bodhichitta isn't so much a matter of study as it is a progressively deeper experience achieved through meditation. When one has some experience of these practices, especially of emptiness, one is prepared for the study and practice of Vajrayana. This is good background information, especially for those new to Vajrayana practice.

To start the study and practice of Vajrayana, one should receive an initiation or empowerment. Any practice you do that doesn't require empowerment is from the sutra system of practice. Any practice that requires initiation belongs to the Vajrayana, or tantra, system. Vajrayana encompasses many skillful methods to realize the nature of emptiness, but they are all based on the study and practice of the sutra system.

When the Buddha gave teachings—or, as it is said, "turned the three wheels of Dharma"—he taught according to the differing dispositions of his audience. All of his vast and profound teachings, both in the sutra system and the tantra system, were taught as remedies to purify the 84,000 types of afflicting emotions that cause suffering. We have to purify each and every one of these 84,000, so the Buddha gave teachings to remedy them all. The sutras and the tantras were not something new that Buddha Shakyamuni invented. They were taught by all the buddhas of the past, and they will also be taught by all the buddhas of the future. Most of the sutra system was taught by Buddha Shakyamuni in his nirmanakaya form. The Vajrayana teachings are mostly taught by buddhas in sambhogakaya forms—for example, Buddha Vairochana and Buddha Vajradhara—to great bodhisattvas, such as Vajrapani. This kind of teaching has never ceased to exist, and it never will. It always exists, but in different places, at different times, and in various forms for different trainees. For example, the Buddha taught in India, and the teachings remained there for several centuries before they were transmitted to and predominantly carried by other countries, such as China and Tibet. Now his teachings are spreading all around the world. The buddhas' activities never cease to exist; they always continue to manifest. On our part, it is very important that we work as much as possible to make a connection to the Buddha and follow the path in order to get the full benefit for ourselves.

You may wonder why there are so many more methods in the tantra system than in the sutra system, even though the objective of both systems is the same—buddhahood. The many methods and skillful means of the tantra system provide more opportunities to dispel ignorance. The tantric practitioner is more advanced, and has greater skill to handle shortcomings and delusions. Through the tantric methods, we can skillfully overcome our obscurations without great hardship. For example, during an initiation, there is an opportunity for the vajra master to explain how to transform our ordinary body, speech, and mind into enlightened body, speech, and mind. But the Vajrayana provides many methods of transformation from the ordinary state to the enlightened state; this is the skillful means of the tantra system. In Vajrayana yidam practice we manifest ourselves in the enlightened state, in which the yidam deity has conquered all delusions. Physically we are transformed into the enlightened state, and perceive phenomena as appearances inseparable from emptiness. Mentally, our afflictions are transformed into emptiness, into wisdom, into uncontrived nonconceptual thought, and so forth. This provides an incomparable opportunity to purify our afflictive emotions and negative karma.

In the Vajrayana system, there are four classes of tantra. They are action tantra, performance tantra, yoga yantra, and unexcelled yoga yantra. These four tantra classes are also related to four different initiations. Every yidam deity has its own particular initiation and meditation practices. Without initiation, one cannot practice the deity's liberated state. But after you receive initiation, you can begin to engage in the liberating meditation practice. There are two parts to the practice: the generation stage and the completion stage.

In the generation stage, you manifest as the enlightened deity in sambhogakaya form, on the basis of bodhichitta, in three ways: with clarity, purity, and confidence.

Generating yourself as the clear appearance of the deity's form, inseparable from the emptiness of the yidam deity, is called clarity.

Then you meditate on the deity's attributes and their meanings, and on the inseparability of their emptiness and appearance; this is called purity. All the attributes, marks, and ornaments of the deity have this nature of purity, and each of them has its own significance. When you understand them all, you understand that the deity's form is not an expression of Tibetan or Indian culture, but an expression of the buddhas' enlightened qualities. Since dharmakaya has the nature of emptiness and luminosity, we ordinary people cannot see its enlightened qualities, but great bodhisattvas can—this is because they can perceive the sambhogakaya forms and they understand the expressions of all the attributes and symbols.

The third aspect of the generation stage is confidence. When you transform into the yidam deity, you should be confident that you actually are the deity. You are a buddha because you have buddha nature. Buddha nature is within all of us, and the Vajrayana methods help us reveal it. This confidence should not be ego-driven arrogance, but a kind of courage based on wisdom that is certainty that you are the deity, inseparable from emptiness and appearance. If you can maintain your yidam form in that state, there is no room for negative thoughts, and no delusions can manifest. This is the practice of the generation stage.

The completion stage has two aspects: with signs and without. Practices with signs include actions such as chanting the mantra, purifying yourself, and purifying all sentient beings. With bodhichitta, we extend our mind to all sentient beings. We send light and mantras everywhere to transform samsara into nirvana and all sentient beings within it into enlightened beings. This purification is the action bodhichitta practice of the Vajrayana system.

More advanced practitioners can practice the generation stage with the six yogas of Naropa: *tummo*, or blazing fire yoga; illusory body; dream yoga; clear light; *phowa*, the transference of consciousness; and bardo, or yoga of the intermediate state. These are special Vajrayana practices that encompass both relative and absolute bodhichitta. Through these methods, we manifest the Buddha's enlightened qualities in order to completely purify all the remaining delusions that have enslaved us and made us suffer throughout the six realms of samsara. We let go of our delusions, as there is no place for them when we manifest the enlightened qualities. These delusions lose their foundation and dissipate. This is the purpose of Vajrayana practice.

The completion without signs stage occurs when the mandala and deities dissolve into emptiness. Practice meditation in this state for as long as you can. These methods, or skillful means, allow the practitioner to attain buddhahood successfully.

It is not enough just to receive the initiation; receiving initiation is just the beginning of Vajrayana practice. It may have allowed us to glimpse what enlightenment is, but we are still not enlightened. In order to achieve enlightenment, we have to follow the complete path, step by step, keeping these precious teachings in our heart. We have to eliminate all our obscurations, which are the causes of suffering. The essential meditation practice is to keep bodhichitta in mind always. The nature of a mind that is imbued with bodhichitta is clear, which keeps the mind peaceful and calm, and brings with it the quality of compassion.

Guru Yoga

After the practice of the yidam comes the very special four-kaya guru yoga. This practice gives us an opportunity to unite our mind with the Buddha's mind gradually. The four-kaya guru yoga practice gives us an opportunity to see the inseparable nature of appearance and emptiness. Several major Buddhist texts, such as the *Treatise on the Unsurpassed Tantra* (*Uttaratantra Shastra*) and the *Ornament of the Mahayana Sutras*, both by Maitreya, contain descriptions of the four kayas, so I recommend their study. Each of the four kayas possesses all of the infinite, perfect qualities of buddhahood: the thirty-two major marks, eighty minor marks, four fearlessnesses, eighteen unique qualities, sixty qualities of melodious speech, and so forth.

When one achieves enlightenment, all the obscurations have been eliminated and the two types of wisdom are fully developed. Once in that state, there is no limit to the activities that can be accomplished to benefit sentient beings and no limit to one's excellent qualities. A buddha can effortlessly emanate infinite manifestations according to the disposition and mental capacity of sentient beings. Even though a buddha has no limits, the appearance of a buddha is generally categorized into four kayas, or bodies: nirmanakaya (emanation body), sambhogakaya (enjoyment body), dharmakaya (truth body), and svabhavikakaya (nature body).

The nirmanakaya appears to ordinary people in a flesh-and-blood form. There are four levels within the nirmanakaya: the supreme emanation body, for example Buddha Shakyamuni, who accomplished the twelve enlightened deeds; the artisan emanation, which appears as a great artist or musician; the inferior emanation, which appears as an animal or other non-human being; and the varied emanation, which can manifest as wind, sound, rain, medicine, and so forth according to the needs of the trainee.

The sambhogakaya manifests for great bodhisattvas who are on the various bhumis, or levels on the path to buddhahood. The buddha manifests according to their level to inspire them to complete their meditation practice so that they eventually attain buddhahood.

The dharmakaya is the absolute state of buddhahood. There is no form to be seen; it is just the nature of wisdom and excellent qualities. In the Vajrayana, we visualize Vajradhara as a personification of the dharmakaya as a skillful method to communicate his attributes.

The svabhavikakaya is the inseparability of all the other three forms.

During a guru yoga session, we practice each of the four kayas, one after another. Before you start this practice, it is important to have a good understanding of the singular nature of the four kayas and to be able to think of them without any contradiction. In addition, it is essential to have developed devotion; that is the key to uniting your mind with that of the guru. With devotion, this four-kaya guru yoga can provide an excellent means to achieve the qualities of perfect buddhahood.

Viewing your guru as the Buddha is a special technique that allows you to receive the complete form of the Buddha's blessings. When you know who the Buddha is, you don't just worship a lifeless statue, but rather you work to unite your mind with the Buddha's mind. For this, you need the living presence of enlightenment in the form of your guru. Your teacher may not actually have all the qualities of a buddha, but you can envision it. The teacher must have those qualities to some extent, at least about 60 percent. Most important is that the teacher have bodhichitta, so that the teacher feels a responsibility to help all sentient beings, especially those who are near to him or her. The students who have such a teacher have a responsibility to connect to the Buddha's mind by envisioning the teacher as the Buddha and then purifying the limitations of their mind. Therefore, we visualize our root teacher as Vajradhara rather than as an ordinary person. Vajradhara is the ultimate buddha, the perfection of purity and all qualities. That creates the best opportunity to develop pure vision so that we can receive all the blessings and enlightened qualities.

Vajradhara Guru Yoga Practice

When we formally enter into retreat, we can perform lengthy practices. But for us with busy lives, that is not practical. So, for those who are interested in at least practicing something, the following is a short Vajradhara guru yoga practice called *Resting the Mind in Its Natural State*, along with some brief instructions.

Refuge and bodhichitta

Visualize Vajradhara situated in space just above and in front of you. He is sitting on the moon and sun disks, which rest on a lotus. He is the embodiment of all the buddhas of the three times. Take refuge and cultivate bodhichitta by reciting this verse three times:

> Lord, precious Buddha of the three times:
> with longing mind, I take refuge one-pointedly in you.
> For the benefit of all mother sentient beings who wander
>   in samsara,

I generate loving-kindness, compassion, and the supreme
mind of enlightenment, bodhichitta.

Visualization

Refresh your visualization of Vajradhara as your root guru. He
is inseparable appearance and emptiness, the embodiment of
all wisdom and compassion, and possesses the perfect qualities of a buddha. Recite this description:

Lord root lama, Vajradhara:
your body, union of appearance and emptiness, shines
    with major and minor marks;
your speech, union of sound and emptiness, resonates
    with divine melodies;
your mind, union of clarity and emptiness, radiates with
    the two omniscient wisdoms.

Mantra recitation

While you are chanting the mantra, infinite light manifests
from Vajradhara and pervades the whole of samsara. Sentient
beings receive blessings from this light, purifying their suffering and the causes of suffering. Repeat this mantra as many
times as you can:

OM AH NAMO GURU VAJRA DRIK MAHA MUDRA
SIDDHI PHALA HUM

Blessing supplication

Here, we are totally devoted to Vajradhara with a one-pointed
mind that yearns to be free from samsara. Say these prayers
without any second thought about aspiring to achieve

enlightenment. Recall that you are trapped in the bondage of karma and afflictions, with waves of suffering manifesting unceasingly. Supplicate Vajradhara, your precious guru on whom you now rely totally. Invoke his wisdom and compassion to help you. Wholeheartedly chant this prayer three times:

> Tightly bound by the iron chains of karma and afflictions, waves of my suffering are unceasing.
> O precious Guru, please look upon me now.
> I have no other refuge but you.

Empowerment and dissolution

After your strong, one-pointed supplication, relax your mind. As you recite the verse below, meditate that white light emanates from Vajradhara's forehead and dissolves into your forehead, purifying all physical obscurations. Thus receive the wisdom body blessing such that your whole body turns into your yidam deity, their appearance and emptiness inseparable. Receive the vase empowerment in this way.

Red light, which is the nature of the buddhas' wisdom speech, emanates from Vajradhara's throat and dissolves into your throat, purifying all obscurations and negative karma associated with speech. Your speech turns into the speech of a buddha, its sound and emptiness inseparable. Receive the secret empowerment in this way.

Blue light, which is the nature of the buddhas' wisdom mind, emanates from Vajradhara's heart and dissolves into your heart, purifying all mental obscurations and afflictions. You realize that your mind is inseparable clarity and emptiness. Receive the wisdom empowerment in this way.

Yellow light emanates from Vajradhara's navel and dissolves into your navel, purifying all the subtle obscurations of your body, speech, and mind. You receive the totality of the mahamudra realization. Receive the fourth empowerment in this way.

Finally, Vajradhara and his seat dissolve into multi-colored, bright light, and that light dissolves into you at the crown of your head. The light pervades your entire body, speech, and mind, purifying all subtle obscurations. Your innate mind is fully revealed as being inseparable from Vajradhara's enlightened mind. All your habitual tendencies are purified, and your mind becomes like space. Rest the mind there in that unborn, unceasing nature. There is nothing to create, nothing to discard. Just be mindful and relaxed for as long as you can.

By the power of this unwavering supplication,
the Guru's immense blessing light shines forth
and dissolves into my body, purifying all obscurations.
The Guru's mind and my mind become inseparable.

Now rest in meditative equipoise.

Dedication

The session concludes with dedication. Bring all of your past, present, and future virtuous deeds, as well as those of all sentient beings and enlightened ones, together with the innate mind into the mandala of your bodhichitta. Then dedicate it all so that every sentient being may actualize this mahamudra meditation, be freed from samsara, and attain enlightenment. Rejoice and feel fortunate. Recite the following verse:

> May all beings who have been my kind mothers and are
>   as numerous as space is vast,
> by the blessing power of meditation and recitation
>   of this prayer
> to the venerated protector of beings, Vajradhara,
> experience the single taste of mahamudra.

Mahamudra

Once we accomplish guru yoga, we can move on to mahamudra itself, which is the total luminosity of mind. Everything manifests from emptiness and everything dissolves into
emptiness. Again, by exercising our mind we can destroy the
delusion and duality of samsara. Within that state we have an
opportunity to uproot all ignorance. Without ignorance, concepts such as attachment, aversion, anger, and so forth, the
root causes of suffering, cannot be found.

Two important methods of practice lead to the experience
of mahamudra, one with an object of focus and one without
an object of focus. First, skill in samadhi, or meditative concentration, is necessary as a foundation. Many methods for
accomplishing samadhi are explained in the mahamudra
texts—following the breath or focusing on an external
object, for example. By using these skillful methods, the gross
thoughts settle down and calmly abide. When one can maintain the mind in equipoise without any object of focus, the
foundation for mahamudra realization has been established.

Both samsara and nirvana are reflections of mind. Samsara reflects a confused mind. One's experience within the
six realms of samsara depends on the degree of one's confusion and the karma that stems from that confused mind. Nir-

vana is also a reflection of mind, but that reflection is based on the absence of confusion. Similarly, the various levels of the enlightened mind—such as shravaka, bodhisattva, or buddha—are based on one's lack of confusion and karma. Thus, though there are many paths one may follow, our sole focus is revelation of the pure mind by eliminating the delusions and adventitious defilements that cause our suffering. There is no need to purify the mind—it has always been pure by itself, uncontrived, unfabricated, and unconditioned, its nature inseparable effulgence and emptiness. Once we reveal it, all our suffering and causes of suffering vanish into emptiness.

Many books have been translated on the subject of mahamudra, so please study them and get teachings from authentic masters before you begin this practice in earnest. Books such as my own translation of Milarepa and Jigten Sumgön's songs of realization called *Opening the Treasure of the Profound* and Tilopa's *Ganges Mahamudra* are two good places to start.

Dedication

As with all practices, we seal whatever merit and virtue we have created by dedicating it to the attainment of complete enlightenment for the benefit of all sentient beings. Some practitioners don't pay much attention to dedication, but it is important for us to understand how to do this practice properly and carefully. As mentioned before, the ultimate goal of these practices is enlightenment. For this we take refuge in the Buddha, Dharma, and Sangha and cultivate bodhichitta, the mind of enlightenment. On those bases, we engage in all our meditation practices and accumulate great merit and wisdom.

These are the accumulations that we should dedicate to the attainment of complete enlightenment. If we dedicate them to fame, success in business, health, or wealth, we will only receive that very limited samsaric benefit. However, if we dedicate all virtues, including our buddha nature, without expectation or attachment, we will definitely achieve our ultimate goal—buddhahood. When we share our accumulations with others, we feel joy, happiness, and freedom because of our generosity. We are skillfully dedicating our body, speech, and mind to all sentient beings.

In a nutshell, no matter what you encounter, you can utilize this fivefold path of mahamudra. Suppose you become ill. That sickness is the result of negative karma, so use it as an opportunity to purify that karma. Instead of just feeling bad, contemplate, "May this sickness purify my negative karma from countless lifetimes." Also consider other sentient beings who are encountering problems with sickness and contemplate, "May this substitute for all the sicknesses and obstacles of sentient beings. May all sentient beings have peace and happiness. May they be free from suffering and attain complete buddhahood." With that thought, manifest yourself and all sentient beings into the yidam. Transform everything into the pure state. Supplicate your guru to give you enough blessings to be able to counteract any obstacles to your meditation practice. Meditate in the state of mahamudra, where everything is perceived as a reflection, a fabrication of karma and your mind. There is nothing substantially real about suffering; it is all emptiness. The whole body is just a collection of dust particles, like a mirage or a bubble. At the end, dedicate all the virtues of this practice to everyone's enlightenment. Everything that happens, whether positive or negative, is an opportunity to enhance your practice of bodhichitta and realization of mahamudra.

We must bring the Dharma into our heart as much as possible to purify our obscurations. We must look at all our shortcomings and, instead of being enslaved by these thoughts, use the Dharma as a tool to purify them. If we can use the Dharma in this way, we will truly benefit and will be much happier. Then we will be able to appreciate the Dharma. Otherwise, it will just turn into a meaningless cultural habit or a superficial display.

Then Anathapindika took the land and Jeta the trees, and they placed them in trust of Sariputta for the Buddha. After the foundations were laid, they began to build the hall which rose loftily in due proportions according to the directions which the Buddha had suggested; and it was beautifully decorated with appropriate carvings. This vihara was called Jetavana, and the friend of the orphans invited the Lord to come to Savatthi and receive the donation. And the Blessed One left Kapilavatthu and came to Savatthi.

While the Blessed One was entering Jetavana, Anathapindika scattered flowers and burned incense, and as a sign of the gift he poured water from a golden dragon decanter, saying, "This Jetavana vihara I give for the use of the brotherhood throughout the world." The Blessed One received the gift and replied: "May all evil influences be overcome; may the offering promote the kingdom of righteousness and be a permanent blessing to mankind in general, to the land of Kosala, and especially also to the benefactor." Then the king Pasenadi, hearing that the Lord had come, went in his royal equipage to the Jetavana vihara and saluted the Blessed One with clasped hands, saying: "Blessed is my unworthy and obscure kingdom that it has met with so great a fortune. For how can calamities and dangers befall it in the presence of the Lord of the World, the Dharmaraja, the King of Truth. Now that I have seen your sacred countenance, let me partake of the refreshing waters of your teachings. Worldly profit is fleeting and perishable, but religious profit is eternal and inexhaustible. A worldly man, though a king, is full of trouble, but even a common man who is holy has peace of mind."

—The Gospel of Buddha

CHAPTER 11

Shravasti: The Four Dharmas of Gampopa

THE MANY RUINS found at Shravasti don't do justice to the former greatness of this city. There are a great many holy sites here because it was one of the central places of the Buddha's teaching career. The ruins are divided into two areas, called Maheth and Saheth. Maheth is the ancient city of Savatthi, as it is referred to in the early Pali texts, the capital of King Prasenajit's realm called Kosala. The ramparts that enclosed the ancient city still stand, forming a mud fortification more than three miles long; four of the city's entrance gates also remain. Excavations began in 1863 and have been nearly continuous since then; numerous terracotta figures and coins have been recovered. One can find stupas in Maheth memorializing Anathapindika, the donor of Jetavana Vihara; Angulimala, the murderer who collected a finger from each of his victims, but who was turned from his destructive path by the Buddha; and King Prasenajit. One of King Ashoka's pillars stood just south of the main site.

For the pilgrim, the more important area is Saheth, about two miles to the southwest. The ruins there are well preserved and accessible. The famous Jetavana Vihara is the highlight. Amid the gardens, monasteries, and stupas are two of the Buddha's residences. The scriptures relate that he spent twenty-five rains retreats here, so visitors are assured of walking in the Buddha's actual footsteps. Ananda's tree is a particularly revered spot. It originated when the Buddha was away one time, and Ananda planted it using a cutting of the Bodhi Tree from Bodh Gaya to serve as a reminder of the Buddha's presence.

Just outside the Jetavana garden are the remains of the Purvarama Monastery that was sponsored by Vishakha, the foremost female patron of the Buddha, who spent six rains retreats there. The spot where Devadatta is said to have fallen into the hell realms is also nearby. Modern temples built by devotees from Sri Lanka, Korea, Myanmar, Cambodia, Thailand, and Tibet are located in the surrounding vicinity to mark this holy site. The most recent addition is the nonsectarian Great Shravasti Buddhist Cultural Assembly, built by His Holiness Drikung Kyabgön Chetsang Rinpoche, throne holder of the Drigung Kagyü lineage, in order to help revive this somewhat underdeveloped area.

Gampopa, the Great Physician

The four Dharmas of Gampopa are a concise summary of the Buddha's many teachings, so it is appropriate to learn about them at the end of our virtual journey through the Buddhist holy sites. Jigten Sumgön, founder of the Drigung Kagyü lineage, said, "The four Dharmas of Gampopa are a complete and unmistaken path that leads to enlightenment. Therefore, one must practice them properly." What good fortune that we are able to study them today! Gampopa was one of the foremost lamas in the history of Tibetan Buddhism. The Buddha predicted his birth and that he would benefit many, many sentient beings. We are still receiving his wisdom and blessings today.

Gampopa was born to religious parents in southern Tibet amid marvelous signs. He first studied the Dharma with his father, and later learned medicine by attending to thirty teachers. He became a widely respected doctor and was nicknamed the "Great Physician." He married at twenty-two and had two children. Unfortunately, his wife and children all passed away at an early age. On her deathbed, his wife said, "There is no happiness in the householder life. After my death, Physician, practice the Dharma wholeheartedly." This event forced him to develop very strong renunciation, and he became a monk.

He excelled in both study and practice within the Kadampa tradition until karma drew him to the extraordinary yogi, Milarepa. Gampopa remained under Milarepa's guidance for three years, during which he studied everything that Milarepa had to teach him—mahamudra, the six yogas of Naropa, and many other tantric teachings. After he attained the greatest realization, he gave countless profound teachings impartially to ordained and lay persons, male and female, old and young, scholars and the illiterate according to each individual's disposition, experience, and interest. He also wrote books that form the foundation for study within the Kagyü lineage, notably *The Jewel Ornament of Liberation* and *A Precious Garland of the Supreme Path*.

The Four Dharmas of Gampopa

The four Dharmas of Gampopa summarize the entire Buddhist path, so they give us a good opportunity to review what this path entails.

It is the nature of sentient beings to want happiness and freedom from suffering, but these goals cannot be achieved merely by wishing—one must employ effective methods to create the causes that will result in happiness. Everything arises in dependence upon causes and conditions, and nothing occurs without a cause, due to an incomplete cause, or because of an unrelated one. Buddhist philosophy clearly explains that karmic causation is inexorable. Simply put, cause and effect operate this way: nonvirtuous thoughts and actions only give rise to suffering, while virtuous thoughts and actions always bring about happiness.

Within the six realms of samsara, peace and happiness are transient and ephemeral. The essence of one's experience in samsara is the suffering of change. Even though we might experience pleasure or even attain great happiness, it is temporary. The only lasting happiness is total freedom from samsara, and this perfect happiness can only be attained through liberation from conditioned existence.

Whether one wishes to achieve complete enlightenment, personal liberation from samsara, or simply temporary happiness, the fundamental practice is to perform the ten virtuous actions and to abandon the ten nonvirtuous actions. Practicing the ten virtuous actions without renunciation of samsara will serve as a cause to be reborn in the higher realms of humans and gods, but one will still not be free from the cycle of suffering. If one practices these same actions based on renunciation of personal suffering, then one will achieve individual liberation. But if one practices them on the basis of bodhichitta, one can achieve buddhahood.

The mind is at the center of the whole system. Even though we cannot see the mind with our eyes, hear it with our ears, or touch it with our body, it is the mind that makes the decision on whether to abide in samsara or in enlightenment. The mind is exceedingly complex and profound. The nature of the mind itself is uncontrived, free from elaboration. The essence of the mind is total peace. Because of this shared quality, everyone desires peace and happiness. It doesn't matter if you are a Buddhist or non-Buddhist, educated or uneducated, rich or poor, human or nonhuman. As long as you have a mind, you will want to be free from suffering.

However, temporary obscurations block the clarity of the mind. This is like the sun's luminosity being covered by clouds. The sun continuously shines brightly, but we cannot always see it because of clouds. Likewise, our mind is always clear, but when it is masked by temporary obscurations, we unwittingly follow negative habitual patterns.

Fortunately, the Buddha completely revealed the nature of the mind free from obscurations, and he taught what he learned without holding anything back. We can still study and practice what he taught with the kind support of teachers and our fellow sangha members. We follow the Buddha not because he was rich and famous, but because of his wisdom and compassion. The Buddha was concerned for the most vulnerable of those suffering—we who are wandering in the desert of delusion. He explained the reality of causality because that is the way the universe functions; we cannot ignore or deny that fact. Our responsibility is to understand that everything happens because of causes and conditions, and then to create the causes of enlightenment for the benefit of all. The Buddha said, "I teach the way to free yourself from suffering. Whether you achieve it is up to you."

In this context, the four Dharmas of Gampopa explain the way to meaningfully implement our desire for happiness in a very succinct way. The four are as follows:

1. Turning the mind to the Dharma
2. The Dharma becoming the path to enlightenment
3. Dispelling error from the path
4. The dawning of confusion as wisdom

They are stated simply, and yet they encompass all teachings of the sutra system and the tantric system.

Sometimes they are expressed as a supplication addressed to the buddhas, great bodhisattvas, and past masters:

1. Grant your blessings so that my mind and all sentient beings' minds turn toward the Dharma
2. Grant your blessings so that the Dharma follows the path
3. Grant your blessings so that mistakes are dispelled from the path
4. Grant your blessings so that confusion dawns into pristine wisdom

It is also helpful to formulate the four Dharmas as an aspiration prayer:

1. May my mind and all sentient beings' minds become the Dharma

2. May the Dharma become the path to enlightenment
3. May all mistakes be dispelled from the path
4. May all confusion arise as wisdom

When you pray this way repeatedly, the four Dharmas are a helpful reminder and also an enhancement for your practice.

1. Turning the Mind to the Dharma

First, let's briefly examine what we mean by "Dharma." In its simplest terms, *Dharma* refers to the teachings of the Buddha. He is the one who discovered the truth of reality and then precisely taught how to become free of suffering. From the Buddha's time to the present, a continuous stream of realized teachers has unerringly passed on the practices and blessings of the Dharma. We are so fortunate that this happened! However, we should be aware that many people call themselves "lamas" these days, and not all of them are authentic teachers. It is important that we investigate the qualifications of those we might accept as teachers; otherwise we could be led in an unproductive—or even detrimental—direction by inauthentic instruction.

The pure Dharma is the method by which we can understand the cause of samsara and the cause of nirvana. It is the means to dispel our mistakes and confusion. The Dharma develops our mind into a wholesome, virtuous state. And, in the end, the Dharma will liberate us from all suffering and enable us to achieve complete, perfect enlightenment. So, weigh the advantages of choosing the Dharma path against the drawbacks of not doing so. Think carefully about which direction leads to happiness and which to suffering. In order to gain certainty in this matter, many find it useful to contemplate the four thoughts that turn the mind to the Dharma. The four thoughts are:

1. Precious human life
2. Impermanence
3. The suffering of samsara
4. Karma

Precious human life

At this moment, we have an opportunity to become completely free from samsara and to achieve complete enlightenment. Animals don't have this capacity, and hungry ghosts and hell beings don't either. Nor do gods or demigods. Even among humans, for a lifetime to be considered a *precious* human rebirth it must possess eighteen qualities of leisure and endowment. As a result, obtaining a precious human life is as rare as a blind turtle swimming in a vast ocean accidently slipping its head through the hole in a floating yoke. Further, this extraordinary circumstance of a precious human life uniquely contains the potential to cross the ocean of samsara, proceed on the path of enlightenment, and attain perfect enlightenment. Taking the time to appreciate this situation is an early step in advancing toward the Dharma.

Impermanence

Next, we turn our attention to impermanence by understanding and contemplating the impermanence of both sentient beings and materials. All phenomena—rocks, cars, clothing, relatives, friends, and oneself—are subject to disintegration. This fact is easy to ignore, but it is true whether we recognize it or not. Whatever we cherish in this life will have to be left behind at the time of death, including one's own body. Picture this clearly in your mind. Death can come anytime; it doesn't matter if you're young and healthy. As the preliminary practice texts say, "Death can descend any time like a drop of morning dew on a blade of grass." Life depends on one short breath. If this breath goes out and doesn't come back, then . . . nothing. Everything we know will be like a passing dream. At that time, what will be of benefit? Only the Dharma. Everything else will be gone. Until this thought is genuinely born in the mind, until we feel it deeply, our understanding will remain merely intellectual, and our mind will not really be following the Dharma. In order for our mind to sincerely turn to the Dharma, this contemplation is necessary. I'm not sharing this to make you uncomfortable. This teaching shows you the truth of samsara and helps you to renounce it.

Suffering of samsara

The suffering of conditioned existence, as we know, involves both physical and mental pain. Sentient beings suffer from not attaining what they strive for, from being separated from what they are attached to, from coming into contact with enemies and other disagreeable conditions, and from being dissatisfied even when they get what they want. We are all caught up in the suffering of misery, the suffering of change, and pervasive suffering. Misery is an experience common to all beings; it is obvious, painful, and dreadful suffering. Change happens continually; things are lost and broken, and precious friends and relatives pass away or turn into enemies. Pervasive suffering is subtler and generally imperceptible to us ordinary beings, yet it is the true nature of our life. There is no part of samsara without suffering. Suffering is the reality of our cyclic existence. Once you become aware of this, you will inevitably seek a way to be free of it. Then, when you discover how the Dharma can purify defilements and lead you to enlightenment, your mind naturally turns in that direction.

Karma

Karma is action—anything that we have done with our body, speech, or mind. Whatever has been done leaves an imprint, positive or negative, on the mind. Eventually, our actions become habits and we follow them without thinking. At the time of death, one's consciousness is driven by karma toward a rebirth that corresponds to our actions. Nonvirtuous actions have negative results, and virtuous actions lead to positive outcomes. Causation is an unstoppable force. Whatever you experience in this life is the result of past karma, just as what you will experience in the future is based on the actions you take now. Thus, if we have a particular goal in mind, then we have no choice but to create the causes that lead to that end. If we yearn for the end of suffering, following the Dharma is our only option. But without deep certainty about the workings of karma, our involvement with the Dharma will be superficial. We will each have to judge for ourselves whether our minds are sincerely turned toward the Dharma, or whether we merely display virtuous appearances for the sake of success in this life.

Sometimes this first of the four Dharmas of Gampopa is expressed as, "May the Dharma become the Dharma." The Buddha taught the unadulterated truth for the benefit of all, but we Buddhists sometimes misuse it. Instead of following the Dharma as a spiritual discipline motivated by bodhichitta, some use it for worldly benefit, such as for gaining fame or wealth. Some make offerings to the highest teachers to enhance their own reputation. They appear devout and go to the temple often, but they only pray for their own good health and increased power. They request empowerments in order to become rich or to make their business more successful. These people are consumed by jealousy, and they constantly evaluate who is more famous, which rival has more wealth, and so on. This means that the Dharma is not "becoming the Dharma." In situations like this, the mind is not following the true Dharma. The real Buddhist teaching, the way the Buddha taught, is to free ourselves and all other beings from suffering—not to create the causes of more suffering. It is of great importance that we avoid misusing the Dharma for improper purposes.

2. The Dharma Becoming the Path to Enlightenment

Many people consider themselves to be true followers of the Buddha, sure that their mind has become one with the holy Dharma. They may, in fact, be influenced by the Dharma, but Gampopa warns us that we must make sure that the Dharma we adopt actually becomes the path to enlightenment. There are many pitfalls.

For the Dharma to become the path, you must cultivate renunciation of samsara. Ordinarily, people focus on this life, doing everything—even spiritual practice—to avoid suffering and experience happiness. They follow the Dharma with the motivation to benefit only themselves. Cherishing oneself above all others is nothing other than the cause of suffering.

Such people may have turned toward the Dharma, but their Dharma has not become a path to enlightenment.

Releasing attachment to samsaric life allows a calm state of mind to arise, which is called *shamatha*, or calm abiding. This form of meditation is a necessary foundation for further progress, but by itself will not free us from samsara. For that, it must be combined with the great wisdom achieved through *vipashyana*, or insight, meditation. When shamatha and vipashyana are synchronized, an individual has a powerful tool with which to uproot delusion. Delusion is basically self-grasping, or grasping at what we identify as "I" or "self." We are so deeply habituated in preserving the ego! This pattern has been acted out lifetime after lifetime, so now it seems impossible to live without this pernicious attachment. But look carefully. Where is that ego? Is it part of your head? Your heart? Try as you might, you cannot see it or hold it in your hand. The self is like a rabbit's horn or a turtle's hair—a nonexistent illusion.

The compassionate Buddha taught that the way to enlightenment is by uprooting delusional beliefs. You cannot achieve it just by saying powerful prayers or by reciting mantras and sutras. The Buddha gave us a practical approach that does not rely on beliefs. The Buddha described the infallible process of causes and results: if you do this, that will result. If you combine shamatha and vipashyana in the right way, freedom from all suffering will result. This is the path we must take to reach our goal.

Does renunciation mean that we have to give up our houses, our family, or our responsibilities and immediately go live in a cave like the famous yogi Milarepa? Is every Buddhist required to become a monk or nun? No, of course not. But we can at least loosen the hold that worldly phenomena have over us. Eight concerns with worldly affairs have been identified, summarized into pairs of hopes and fears:

1. Hope of gain and fear of loss
2. Hope of pleasure and fear of pain
3. Hope of fame and fear of disgrace
4. Hope of praise and fear of blame

When we reflect on these, we find that we are already quite familiar with them in our lives, so I don't need to explain these to you. What is important is that we recognize their influence over us. If we spend our time studying and practicing this kind of dharma, so to speak, then we would not be following the path to enlightenment. Rather, we would be going further and deeper into samsara. Real happiness starts to arise when we forego attachment to material objects, temporary pleasures, our reputation, and hearing nice words. Look again at the four thoughts that turn the mind, especially impermanence, and make an effort to renounce samsaric concerns in order to follow the path toward enlightenment. We can't travel on two paths at the same time.

What should we adopt instead? How do we give up this self-defeating perspective? We must shift our focus away from ourselves and toward others. Genuinely cultivate the wish that other sentient beings have happiness and the causes of happiness. Sincerely hope for all sentient beings to be free from suffering and the causes of suffering. This attitude will lead to real harmony. In order to achieve external harmony, we must first achieve harmony within our own mind by eliminating confusion, ignorance, anger, hatred, and attachment. With this as our main practice, we can be sure that our practice is following the right path. If we continue to develop afflicting emotions, ego, and anger, then our practice is going in the wrong direction.

The study and practice of loving-kindness and compassion are not only important in the spiritual field, but also in daily life. Some think that practicing compassion means becoming a passive, weak person. The truth is just the opposite. The more you practice loving-kindness and compassion, the more you will build strength in the mind. Loving-kindness and compassion form the real path to transforming a negative environment into a positive one. The less compassion and loving-kindness are present, the weaker the mind. A weak mind is easily agitated by anger and aggression, but the moment we have an attitude of loving-kindness and compassion, peace and harmony result.

Recall that on the basis of loving-kindness and compassion, we can start to cultivate the mind of enlightenment, or bodhichitta. This path is infallible; all the buddhas and bodhisattvas of the past achieved realization by developing bodhichitta, and all the buddhas and bodhisattvas of the future will do likewise. There are none who have achieved realization without it. As we know, there are two categories of bodhichitta: the absolute and the relative. Absolute bodhichitta is concerned with realizing the nature of all phenomena or the nature of the mind, and entails the study and practice of mahamudra or dzogchen. Relative bodhichitta is further divided into two: aspirational and action bodhichitta. In *Engaging in the Bodhisattva's Way of Life*, Shantideva likens aspirational bodhichitta to a desire to travel to a certain place, while action bodhichitta is said to be like taking steps toward actually traveling there. Thus, aspiration bodhichitta is a wish, and action bodhichitta is actual effort toward making the wish a reality.

It may not be possible for us to put our aspirations regarding loving-kindness, compassion, and bodhichitta into action right away. First, we must establish these attitudes firmly in the mind. Unless we develop the mind before we act, our actions will be very limited because we will be easily discouraged. Your initial enthusiasm for acting with loving-kindness or bodhichitta can dissipate quickly, and when you lose that enthusiasm, you will not be able to bring forth the effort to stay on the path. Therefore, serious reflection is necessary for the Dharma to become one's path. On the other hand, with a strong mind we will be able to persevere no matter what difficulties we have to endure.

Watch your mind to gauge how your practice is coming along, and whether it is successful. Is your mind becoming smoother and more relaxed? Is there is more spaciousness and less aggression? If so, then the Dharma is becoming a path to enlightenment. If these changes are not happening, then even our so-called spiritual practice can cause us to become more arrogant. We might brag about how many mantras we've recited or congratulate ourselves on how many prostrations we have done. We are more likely to develop pride about the length of time we can sit in meditation posture. Unless we are motivated by benefitting others, the Dharma will cause us to develop a stronger ego. In that case, the Dharma is clearly being misused to advance samsara rather than defeat it.

3. Dispelling Error from the Path

No matter what kind of practice we do from which tradition, our main focus should be on eliminating the three poisons—ignorance, desire, and aversion. If, in the name of the Dharma, we develop desire or other afflictions, then we are just becoming more deeply enmeshed in samsara. When we study and practice the Dharma we must watch our own mind. If our mind is becoming more clear, open, calm, patient, aware, and understanding, then that is a sign that error is being dispelled from the path. If, on the other hand, we are becoming more arrogant, undisciplined, confused, and hardened, and we see only negative qualities in others, then error is not being dispelled from the path—even if we appear to practice advanced Dharma teachings such as the Vajrayana. In order to practice successfully, we must always recall the four thoughts that turn the mind, loving-kindness, compassion, and bodhichitta, and maintain awareness of interdependence. The revered Jigten Sumgön said that preliminary points such as these are much more profound and important than the advanced practices. Without a firm foundation in these preliminaries, advanced practices such as tantra and mahamudra will not be effective.

You yourself know how hard it is to change your mind. It is like stretching a rubber band; when you release the band, it goes right back to its original shape. Sometimes you feel so much compassion that tears come to your eyes. You understand that everyone needs loving-kindness and compassion and feel a strong pull to practice them, but as soon as you return to your daily life, you go back to your old self-centered habits. These habits are deeply rooted, so we must remind ourselves of the Dharma teachings again and again and again. That is the real practice—something we do twenty-four hours a day, not just sitting on a cushion for a few minutes, only to forget what we practiced soon after.

We say we want to help all sentient beings, that we want them all to be free from suffering. We also want to cultivate bodhichitta and to achieve buddhahood. However, at present, we do not have the ability or strength to bring these things about. Our mind is completely under the control of the three poisons. The only path to purification of these three poisons consists of loving-kindness, compassion, and bodhichitta. When you have love for all sentient beings, your attachment to only certain individuals will be purified because you will love all equally. When you have compassion for all sentient beings, your anger will be purified because you will see how they are suffering because of their delusion.

Practicing loving-kindness and compassion is the best way to heal the mind, which has been wounded by afflictions. It will definitely cause your mind to recover because we all have the seed of enlightenment, which is buddha nature. We are like raw diamonds, which are not useful as ornaments, but contain every potential. Individuals who can recognize a raw diamond will polish it and cut it until it becomes a valued jewel. Likewise, it is our responsibility to "polish" our buddha nature so that we become useful to all beings. The Buddha taught us everything we need to know; all we have to do is implement his advice. We are so fortunate to have this opportunity to purify all the obscurations that block our buddha nature. Thus, we undertake the unerring path of the six perfections with confidence and joy. We make an unyielding commitment to purification and to the development of the qualities of a bodhisattva and, eventually, those of a buddha.

The six perfections are designed to ensure unerring progress on the path to enlightenment. In fact, the practice of the six perfections is indispensable to perfecting bodhichitta and attaining complete enlightenment. They constitute the action called for in the term "action bodhichitta." The six, which are described very skillfully in Gampopa's *Jewel Ornament of*

Liberation, are generosity, moral ethics, patience, perseverance, meditative concentration, and wisdom.

Generosity

As we know, generosity is listed first among the six perfections because it is easiest one to develop naturally. Generosity, the act of giving, lessens our attachment and builds our store of merit. Generosity is more than giving wealth. There are many opportunities to reduce our confusion and suffering through giving, such as giving wealth, health, freedom from fear, and Dharma teachings, as well as supporting those who are in trouble or pain. It is important not to ruin this practice with improper generosity, such as giving in order to cause harm, offering stolen property, providing something that increases the recipient's negativity, or giving with arrogance. Take care to give appropriate items with a good motivation to suitable recipients.

If you approach this practice with high expectations, it will be easy to become disappointed or discouraged. When others don't appreciate your generosity or are resentful or just uninterested, your expectation of recognition will make you suffer. You may feel that your practice of generosity is pointless and without benefit, and so stop doing it. It is much better to release such expectations. Simply share what you have with others. A sincere, altruistic motivation frees you from the expectation that others will respond positively to what you do. The act of giving is itself great Dharma practice. Nothing more is needed.

Moral ethics

The second quality to perfect is moral ethics, sometimes referred to as discipline. What makes morality Buddhist? It starts with an understanding of causality—that is, knowing with certainty that all actions have results. In particular, it is seeing that positive actions lead to positive results, and negative actions have proportionately negative results. Thus, all virtuous thoughts and actions are encouraged and all nonvirtuous thoughts and actions are to be purified.

Moral discipline is important from the beginning to the highest levels of tantric practice. Morality is the foundation from which we can reduce and purify our three poisons. To summarize, morality comes in three types of practice, depending on the ability of the practitioner: restraint, accumulation of virtuous deeds, and benefitting sentient beings. The first one means to stop creating harm and performing nonvirtuous deeds. Taking and keeping vows is an especially fruitful aspect of this practice. Where restraint can be thought of as actions to avoid, accumulating virtues consists of taking positive actions. This can be done in an infinite number of ways, such as studying Dharma, sharing your Dharma knowledge, attending to spiritual masters, moderate eating and sleeping, making offerings, and giving to the needy. When you are fully established in bodhichitta, you can turn your attention to helping others by protecting them, inspiring them, repaying their kindness, and generally dispelling their suffering by leading them to enlightenment.

In particular, we speak of the ten nonvirtues and ten virtues as the heart of Buddhist morality. The ten nonvirtues and ten virtues, their opposites, are as follows:

1. Refraining from killing, and preserving life
2. Refraining from stealing, and practicing generosity
3. Refraining from sexual misconduct, and practicing moral ethics
4. Refraining from lying, and speaking truthfully
5. Refraining from divisive speech, and speaking harmoniously
6. Refraining from harsh words, and speaking peacefully and politely
7. Refraining from idle talk, and speaking meaningfully
8. Refraining from covetousness, and practicing contentment
9. Refraining from malice, and practicing lovingkindness and compassion
10. Refraining from holding wrong views, and practicing the perfect meaning

These ten virtues are not a Buddhist belief; they are not virtuous just because the Buddha said so. They are universal. If you practice the ten virtues and avoid the ten nonvirtues anywhere, even in places that have no religion at all, the people there will appreciate it and rejoice. It doesn't matter whether they are Buddhists or even if they don't believe anything; these actions are moral because the ten nonvirtues cause suffering and the ten virtues cause peace and happiness without fail.

Patience
The third perfection, patience, has to do with developing strength in the mind, with building the mind up to be like a mountain that cannot be moved by the wind of negative forces. Our whole world is occupied with mental afflictions.

For instance, simply look at how we are constantly bombarded by advertising; all these ads are trying to do is increase your attachment. If only you had such-and-such product, your life would be better, your health would improve, and all your troubles would magically go away. We need the Buddha's wisdom to withstand samsara's assaults and reduce the afflictions.

Patience is a very useful practice for encountering difficulty; it keeps us from reacting with anger, resentment, or harm. Patience protects our peace of mind and helps us endure hardship. While the practice of patience is related to all the afflicting emotions, it is most directly associated with anger. When anger arises, we should learn to work with it, minimize it, and eventually uproot it. Instead of automatically placing blame on others, investigate the complete circumstances of the situation. Shantideva suggests that the one angering you has no choice; anger is in control, not the individual, so there is no reason to retaliate. Recall that you cannot be harmed unless you had previously created the cause, so the harm you are experiencing is the result of your own karma—again, no reason to become angry with someone else. You can also use patience to strengthen your understanding of emptiness by thinking that there is actually no harm, no one causing harm, and so forth. As a bodhisattva, you have vowed to benefit *all* beings, including the one criticizing you, so think about how inappropriate it would be to harm anyone, even one who has harmed you.

Patience can be an important aspect of meditation practice, too. Sometimes the mind is not clear, and other times we cannot visualize well. We encounter physical pain from sitting, especially in the knees and back. Finding time for meditation can cause us stress. It can seem like we are making no progress at all, so we might be tempted to give it up. Having patience will help us get through such obstacles. Read the inspiring life stories of great masters of the past, such as Milarepa, and consider what they endured. No matter what happened, they continued on the path. Think, "Shouldn't I be more like them?" Other people risk their life engaging in dangerous sports for no purpose other than entertainment. Meditation practice, progressing toward freedom from suffering, working to achieve enlightenment—these are goals worth sacrificing for. At the same time, patience doesn't mean you torture yourself. We need to apply wisdom and skill to determine whether patience is appropriate in a particular situation. Going through meaningless suffering will not help us achieve anything. No one achieves enlightenment by way of the hell realms; suffering will not help us become free of suffering. We must use patience to accumulate merit and develop wisdom, not to waste our time. Use patience to reduce the energy of your negative thoughts, your anger, and your attachment. This is not an easy thing.

Perseverance

Perseverance, or joyous effort, supports all the other perfections. Dharma practice means removing confusion and delusion from our mind—in other words, dispelling error and despair from our path. This is essential once you have taken the Dharma as your path. We must practice Dharma step by step every day without fail, and we need perseverance to do so.

Perseverance is built up from an appreciation of the Dharma teachings. Because they are so precious and so holy, we also become precious and holy when we apply them in our mind. Consider the buddhas and bodhisattvas who we admire and respect so much. The Dharma teachings are what made them great. When we deeply feel that the Dharma is marvelous and the most important thing in our life, we can practice joyfully without hesitation. Even when we face some problems, we can still continue with joy as long as we don't lose sight of the preciousness of the Dharma.

Perseverance helps protect us from all types of laziness: listlessness, procrastination, making excuses, discouragement, distraction, and attachment to evil ways, for example. These attitudes keep us from making spiritual progress, and can even turn us away from our chosen path. Perseverance instills in us an unshakable commitment to all beings, which makes it impossible to turn away. It encourages us to be diligent in abandoning nonvirtuous deeds and adopting virtuous ones, to be mindful of our thoughts and actions in every moment, to endure the challenges of samsara without aversion, and to live among its pleasures without attachment. In short, to be relentless in our advance toward buddhahood.

Meditative concentration

The fifth perfection is called samadhi in Sanskrit, and can be translated as meditative concentration, meditative absorption, or meditative equipoise. Basically, it is stability of the mind. In ordinary life, our mind is generally scattered here and there among concerns such as our job, our family, preparing food, our body, traffic, entertainment, spending and saving money, and so forth. We live completely within the grasp of the afflicting emotions. Life is so hectic that there is little room left for spiritual effort.

On the other hand, when the mind is calm, we feel free. When the mind is clear, we can reflect on the Dharma easily and start to penetrate its profound depths. Attachments and aversions will naturally fall away when the mind is stable, and will be replaced with virtue, compassion, loving-kindness, and wisdom. In fact, it is essential to establish the mind in stability in order to gain the special insight that leads to wisdom awareness.

Achieving samadhi may seem impossible, but if you practice even a little each morning and evening, you can slowly bring your mind to the right place. Take a deep breath. Let the gross mental activities subside. Recall that everything is impermanent; suffering is everywhere. Encourage a sense of compassion and loving-kindness to develop. You'll find that you're able to handle things more carefully, peacefully. Mindfulness of your thoughts and actions will improve. A controlled mind is itself a state of ease and happiness; there is no need to search outside.

There are many, many types and methods of meditation—far too numerous to discuss here. However, various texts such as *The Jewel Ornament of Liberation* can give us helpful advice about how to dispel errors from our path. To mention just a few examples:

- If you are disturbed by anger, focus your meditation on loving-kindness.
- If you are disturbed by attachment, focus more on impermanence.
- If you are disturbed by jealousy, try the practice of equalizing yourself and others.
- If you are disturbed by pride, the practice of exchanging yourself and others is useful.
- If you are disturbed by ignorance, concentrate on interdependent origination.

- If you are disturbed by scattered thoughts, train in watching the breath.
- If you are disturbed by mental suffering, meditate on the emptiness of the cause of the problem.

Wisdom

The final perfection is wisdom, the mind that penetrates the nature of phenomena and realizes the nature of the mind. This wisdom is the antidote for the ignorance at the heart of samsara. With it, one can distinguish the way phenomena appear and function (i.e., relative reality) from the true nature of phenomena (i.e., ultimate reality). It unerringly understands the universal causes of suffering and happiness.

In order to penetrate this meaning beyond a superficial or intellectual understanding, it is not sufficient just to reflect on impermanence, the suffering that is the nature of life, and the causes and effects that make up karma. These contemplations, along with the perfections discussed above, are indeed beneficial. But to cut through our delusion, to actually end suffering and attain enlightenment, special insight is necessary.

The true nature of existence and our common perception of it are completely different. Commonly, we perceive our experiences as "real"—we exist, pain and pleasure are substantial, material objects are tangible, and so forth. We are so completely enmeshed in samsara that we do not question whether such a perception of reality is accurate. However, we must resist the conception that these things exist inherently, that they exist exclusively from their own side without reliance on any other factors. In truth, they are interdependent. For example, a cup of tea does not magically appear on your table by itself alone. No, someone grew the tea in dependence on land, water, and sunlight. Someone picked the leaves, dried them, shipped them, packaged them, and so on, until the tea leaves were soaked in hot water and made into the palatable drink before you. Many causes and conditions came together to result in that cup of tea. By thus analyzing materials as being nothing more than a collection of parts, our insistence on their solidity starts to fade. When this sort of analysis is carried to greater lengths, we can perceive all of reality—including ourselves—as being like a mirage, a rainbow, a bubble, a dream, or an illusion. Our mistaken perceptions inevitably lead us to attachment, aversion, and suffering. When the mind starts to see reality clearly and accurately, genuine freedom begins.

4. The Dawning of Confusion as Wisdom

It is an essential Mahayana teaching that buddha nature completely pervades all sentient beings. This means that buddhahood requires nothing from outside ourselves; there is no quality or skill that we do not already have. Thus, our study and practice of the Dharma is for the purpose of recognizing the ultimate mode of abiding of all phenomena, the reality of the primordial state. If we continue to develop more ignorance, desire, and aversion, confusion cannot dawn as wisdom. We cannot achieve buddhahood with afflicting emotions, only by purifying these defilements. This has been emphasized by all the great masters of the past.

When we speak of confusion and wisdom, there are two entities, a duality. Gampopa seems to be saying that one thing (confusion) transforms into another thing (wisdom) or that the essential nature of confusion somehow changes and becomes the nature of wisdom. That isn't what is meant by this fourth Dharma statement. In the advanced Buddhist teachings, we come to realize that the very confusion that causes our suffering is the nature of wisdom; confusion and wisdom are nondual. Nonduality is a difficult concept to express in any language; this Dharma statement has been variously translated as "error arising into wisdom," "confusion dawning as wisdom," and "confusion dawning into primordial wisdom." Nagarjuna expressed the same idea when he said, "There is no distinction whatsoever between saṃsāra and nirvāṇa. There is no distinction whatsoever between nirvāṇa and saṃsāra."[9]

As they have been preserved in Tibet, the Buddha's teachings approach this realization gradually and systematically by working with the afflicting emotions. Through meditation, we learn to recognize these emotions and build our strength to minimize them. Step by step, we purposefully reduce our anger, attachment, greed, and so forth. Then we apply specific antidotes, as described earlier—for example, practicing loving-kindness to counteract anger or using interdependent origination to reduce ignorance. Later on, we use tantric methods like visualization to transform this ordinary state into the enlightened state. According to our ability, we experience ourselves and all sentient beings as deities and then carry that experience onto the path. This technique of taking the result—that is, the enlightened state—as the path is so characteristic of tantra that Vajrayana is sometimes called the "fruition" or "resultant" vehicle. After becoming experienced in this, one will no longer need to avoid or transform the afflicting emotions. Rather, the afflictions are fully realized as wisdom.

How do we go about accomplishing such a profound and subtle state of mind? We use the mind to go within and discover the clarity of mind. For example, look at whether you yourself exist and whether others exist. So long as we think they exist, there is duality: self and other, samsara and nirvana, happiness and suffering, buddhas and sentient beings. We examine the mind closely because the only place to find buddhahood is within your own mind. Is there actually one mind or two? Where is the mind? What color is it? What is its shape and size? Where do thoughts come from and where do they go? We cannot be satisfied with others' explanations and descriptions, but must experience precise determinations of the answers for ourselves. One who understands the nature of the mind, who has seen the ultimate truth, destroys dualistic grasping. The afflictions dissipate into a nondual state. This is how confusion dawns as wisdom.

For those of you who are interested in following the path of Dharma, it is necessary to practice sincerely and with mindfulness. Intellectually understanding the Dharma is not so difficult. What is difficult is practicing it. Without a proper method of practice, there will be little sign of progress. Laziness is deeply ingrained and it always causes us to postpone practice. The current of negative propensities is very strong, and it sweeps us along without choice. Letting ourselves become slaves to our merciless negative thoughts, we suffer unnecessarily. The Dharma is the only means by which we can free ourselves, but it must be practiced with mindfulness and sincerity. If we do not abandon the Dharma, the Dharma will never abandon us. Dharma is the real refuge that can lead us to buddhahood.

A Guru Yoga that Brings the Dharmakaya onto the Path

kön chok kun dü la ma dor je chang jang chup
bar du mi drel kyab su chi
Vajradhara Lama, embodiment of the Three Jewels,
I take refuge in you,
and will until I attain enlightenment.

trul nang du ke nar wa'i dro wa nam
mi ne sa la gö chir sem kyé do
Sentient beings, victims of the confused projection that is
     suffering,
I generate the mindset for enlightenment
in order to establish you all in the nonabiding state.

dor je chang wang jig ten sum gön shab
top chu mi jig ma dre den la shug
jam tsé sem chok tsen be ö ser tro
trin lé tok me dro wa'i tha dang nyam

Lord Vajradhara Jigten Sumgön sits on a seat of the ten
   strengths,
four fearlessnesses, and eighteen unique dharmas;
with major and minor marks of love, compassion, and
   bodhichitta radiating rays of light; and
nonconceptual enlightened activities reaching all migrators
   equally.

om ah ratna shri sarva siddhi hum
OM AH RATNA SHRI SARVA SIDDHI HUM

de dü lu rik drön dang mar mé dzé
ma ong cham pa da ta shak ya thup
lu drup lar trul nyam mé rin chen pal
jig ten sum gön shab la sol wa deb
You are the buddhas Nagakulapradipa and Dipankara
   of the past,
Maitreya of the future, and Shakyamuni of the present;
the reincarnation of Nagarjuna; the peerless Ratna Shri—
Lord Jigten Sumgön, I supplicate you.

la ma'i ku sung thuk lé ö ser trö
dak gi né shir thim pé drip shi dak
wang shi lek thop ku shi sa bön trun
la ma rang thim rang sem sal tong ngang
Light rays emanate from the guru's body, speech, and mind
   and dissolve into my four places,
thereby purifying the four obscurations, bestowing the four
   empowerments,
and planting the seeds of the four kayas.

The guru then dissolves into me.
My mind is natural luminosity-emptiness.

khor dé dü sum sak yö ge tshog kyi
dak dang kha nyam sem chen ma lü pa
dön dam lhan chik kyé pa'i dön tok te
si shir mi né thar chin sa thop shok
Through both the innate virtue
and the virtue accumulated in the three times by all in
    samsara and nirvana,
may I and all sentient beings filling space, none left out,
realize the coemergent ultimate reality and
attain the final state of nonabidance in existence or peace.

APPENDIX B

The *Heart Sutra*

The Blessed Mother, the Heart of the Perfection of Wisdom[10]
In Sanskrit: *Bhagavati Prajna Paramita Hridaya*

Thus have I once heard:
The Blessed One was staying in Rajgriha at Vulture Peak along with a great community of monks and a great community of bodhisattvas, and at that time, the Blessed One entered the meditative absorption on the varieties of phenomena called the appearance of the profound. At that time as well, the noble Avalokiteshvara, the bodhisattva, the great being, clearly beheld the practice of the profound perfection of wisdom itself and saw that even the five aggregates are empty of intrinsic existence.

Thereupon, through the Buddha's inspiration, the venerable Shariputra spoke to the noble Avalokiteshvara, the bodhisattva, the great being, and said, "How should any noble son or noble daughter who wishes to engage in the practice of the profound perfection of wisdom train?"

When this had been said, the holy Avalokiteshvara, the bodhisattva, the great being, spoke to the venerable Shariputra and said, "Shariputra, any noble son or noble daughter who so wishes to engage in the practice of the profound perfection of wisdom should clearly see this way: they should see perfectly that even the five aggregates are empty of intrinsic existence. Form is emptiness, emptiness is form; emptiness is not other than form, form too is not other than emptiness. Likewise, feelings, perceptions, mental formations, and consciousness are all empty. Therefore, Shariputra, all phenomena are emptiness; they are without defining characteristics; they are not born, they do not cease; they are not defiled, they are not undefiled; they are not deficient, and they are not complete.

"Therefore, Shariputra, in emptiness there is no form, no feelings, no perceptions, no mental formations, and no consciousness. There is no eye, no ear, no nose, no tongue, no body, and no mind. There is no form, no sound, no smell, no taste, no texture, and no mental objects. There is no eye-element and so on up to no mind-element including up to no element of mental consciousness. There is no ignorance, there is no extinction of ignorance, and so on up to no aging and death and no extinction of aging and death. Likewise, there is no suffering, origin, cessation, or path; there is no wisdom, no attainment, and even no non-attainment.

"Therefore, Shariputra, since bodhisattvas have no attainments, they rely on this perfection of wisdom and abide in it. Having no obscuration in their minds, they have no fear, and by going utterly beyond error, they will reach the end of nirvana. All the buddhas too who abide in the three times attained the full awakening of unexcelled, perfect enlightenment by relying on this profound perfection of wisdom.

"Therefore, one should know that the mantra of the perfection of wisdom—the mantra of great knowledge, the unexcelled mantra, the mantra equal to the unequalled, the mantra that quells all suffering—is true because it is not deceptive. The mantra of the perfection of wisdom is proclaimed:

TADYATHA GATÉ GATÉ PARAGATÉ PARASAMGATÉ BODHI SVAHA

Shariputra, the bodhisattvas, the great beings, should train in the perfection of wisdom in this way."

Thereupon, the Blessed One arose from that meditative absorption and commended the holy Avalokiteshvara, the bodhisattva, the great being, saying this is excellent. "Excellent! Excellent! O noble child, it is just so; it should be just so. One must practice the profound perfection of wisdom just as you have revealed. For then even the tathagatas will rejoice."

As the Blessed One uttered these words, the venerable Shariputra, the holy Avalokiteshvara, the bodhisattva, the great being, along with the entire assembly, including the worlds of gods, humans, asuras, and gandharvas, all rejoiced and hailed what the Blessed One had said.

Translated by Thupten Jinpa

Seventeen Stages of Samadhi

Arupadhatu: Formless Realm

Naivasamjnanasamjna ayatana: Sphere of neither perception nor nonperception
Akinchanya ayatana: Sphere of nothing whatsoever
Vijnananantya ayatana: Sphere of infinite consciousness
Akashanantya ayatana: Sphere of infinite space

Rupadhatu: Form Realm

Fouth level of dhyana meditation
Third level of dhyana meditation
Second level of dhyana meditation
First level of dhyana meditation

Kamadhatu: Desire Realm

Chittasthapana: Initial placement
Chittapravahasamsthapa: Continual placement
Chittapratiharana: Patchy placement

Chittopasthapana: Close placement
Chittadamana: Subdued placement
Chittasamana: Pacified placement
Chittavyupasamana: Completely pacified placement
Chittaikotikarana: Single-pointed
Samadhana: Complete equipoise

Glossary of Enumerations

Two

accumulations
1. merit
2. wisdom

kayas (bodies of a buddha)
1. rupakaya (form body)
2. dharmakaya (wisdom body)

rupakayas (form bodies of a buddha)
1. sambhogakaya (enjoyment body)
2. nirmanakaya (emanation body)

stages of tantric practice
1. generation or arising stage
2. completion or perfection stage

truths
1. relative truth
2. absolute truth

types of selflessness
1. personal self
2. self of phenomena

types of wisdom
1. the wisdom of knowing reality as it is
2. the wisdom of knowing everything

Three
aspects of generation stage practice
1. clarity
2. purity
3. confidence

higher trainings
1. morality (*shila*)
2. meditative concentration (*samadhi*)
3. wisdom (*prajna*)

knowledges of a buddha
1. knowledge of past lives, his own and all other beings
2. knowledge of the operation of karma, cause and effect
3. knowledge that he is truly and completely free of all
   obscurations and obstacles

jewels
1. Buddha
2. Dharma
3. Sangha

pitakas (divisions of Buddhist scripture)
1. Vinaya
2. Sutra
3. Abhidharma

poisons
1. ignorance
2. desire or attachment
3. anger or aversion

realms
1. desire
2. form
3. formless

times
1. past
2. present
3. future

types of suffering
1. suffering of suffering
2. suffering of change
3. pervasive or conditioned suffering

vehicles
1. hearer
2. solitary realizer
3. bodhisattva

Four

abandonments

1. abandoning nonvirtuous actions that had been taken up
2. not developing new nonvirtues
3. adopting new virtues that had not previously arisen
4. perfecting virtues that have arisen

activities

1. peaceful
2. increasing
3. magnetizing
4. wrathful

classes of tantra

1. action tantra (*kriyatantra*)
2. performance tantra (*charyatantra*)
3. yoga tantra (*yogatantra*)
4. unexcelled yoga tantra (*anuttarayogatantra*)

elements

1. earth
2. water
3. fire
4. wind

empowerments

1. vase
2. secret
3. wisdom
4. fourth or word

extreme views

1. existence
2. nonexistence
3. neither existence nor nonexistence
4. both existence and nonexistence

fearlessnesses (of a buddha)

1. certainty that all obscurations without exception have been purified and all defilements exhausted
2. certainty that all complete and perfect qualities have been actualized
3. certainty that all obstacles have been identified as such and purified
4. certainty of having taught the methods that will produce enlightenment

foundations of miracle powers

1. absorption of aspiration
2. absorption of perseverance
3. absorption of meditation
4. absorption of investigation that develops precision of mind in the meditative state

kayas (forms of a buddha)

1. the emanation body (*nirmanakaya*)
2. the complete enjoyment body (*sambhogakaya*)
3. the perfect wisdom body (*dharmakaya*)
4. the basis for the manifestation of the other three forms (*svabhavikakaya*)

main pilgrimage sites
1. Lumbini (Buddha's birthplace)
2. Bodh Gaya (seat of enlightenment)
3. Sarnath (site of first teaching)
4. Kushinagar (site of parinirvana)

mindfulnesses
1. mindfulness of the body as impermanent and subject to decay
2. mindfulness of feelings—joy, suffering, and neutral feelings—as being transitory
3. mindfulness of mind as being like a cloud
4. mindfulness of phenomena as being interdependent

noble truths
1. truth of suffering
2. truth of the cause of suffering
3. truth of the cessation of suffering
4. truth of the path (the noble eightfold path)

Five
aggregates. See *skandhas*

fivefold path of mahamudra
1. bodhichitta
2. deity yoga
3. guru yoga
4. mahamudra
5. dedication of merit

lay precepts

1. abstaining from killing
2. abstaining from consuming intoxicants
3. abstaining from sexual misconduct
4. abstaining from stealing
5. abstaining from wrong speech

paths

1. path of accumulation
2. path of application
3. path of insight
4. path of meditation
5. path of perfection

powers

1. power of faith
2. power of perseverance
3. power of mindfulness
4. power of absorption
5. power of wisdom awareness

skandhas (aggregates)

1. form
2. feeling
3. perception
4. mental formation
5. consciousness

strengths

1. strength of faith
2. strength of perseverance

3. strength of mindfulness

4. strength of absorption

5. strength of wisdom awareness

types of clairvoyance

1. knowing others' thoughts

2. clairaudience

3. knowledge of former lifetimes

4. knowledge of the future

5. miracle powers

Six

perfections (paramitas)

1. generosity

2. moral ethics

3. patience

4. perseverance

5. meditative concentration

6. wisdom awareness

realms

1. hell realm

2. hungry ghost realm

3. animal realm

4. human realm

5. demigod realm

6. god realm

yogas of Naropa

1. tummo

2. illusory body

3. dream yoga

4. clear light

5. phowa

6. bardo

Seven

branches of enlightenment

1. perfect mindfulness

2. perfect discrimination

3. perfect perseverance

4. perfect joy

5. perfect relaxation

6. perfect absorption

7. perfect equanimity

Eight

eightfold path

1. perfect view

2. perfect conception

3. perfect speech

4. perfect action

5. perfect livelihood

6. perfect effort

7. perfect mindfulness

8. perfect absorption

great pilgrimage sites

1. Lumbini (birthplace of the Buddha)

2. Bodh Gaya (place of enlightenment)

3. Sarnath (place where the four noble truths were taught)

4. Kushinagar (place of parinirvana)

5. Shravasti (place of a miracle display)
6. Rajgir (place where Nalagiri, the elephant, was subdued)
7. Sankassa (place where the Buddha descended to earth from Trayastrimsha Heaven)
8. Vaishali (place of receiving an offering of honey from a monkey)

leisures
(freedom from these eight unfavorable conditions:)
1. being born in a hell realm
2. being born a hungry ghost
3. being born an animal
4. being born a barbarian
5. being born a long-lived god
6. holding wrong views
7. absence of a buddha
8. muteness

worldly concerns
1. gain
2. loss
3. fame
4. disgrace
5. comfort
6. pain
7. criticism
8. praise

Ten
bhumis (stages of a bodhisattva)
1. Great Joy

2. Stainless
3. Radiant
4. Luminous
5. Very Difficult to Train
6. Obviously Transcendent
7. Gone Afar
8. Immovable
9. Good Discriminating Wisdom
10. Cloud of Dharma

endowments
(five personal conditions:)
 1. being human
 2. being born in a central country
 3. possessing all the senses
 4. having committed none of the heinous actions
 5. having devotion for the Dharma
(five external conditions:)
 6. a buddha has appeared
 7. a buddha has taught
 8. the Dharma that was taught remains
 9. there are practitioners of the Dharma
 10. there is love and kind support for practice

nonvirtues
(three of body)
 1. taking
 2. stealing
 3. sexual misconduct
(four of speech)
 4. lying

5. divisive speech
6. harsh words
7. idle talk
(three of mind)
8. covetousness
9. aversion
10. wrong view

strengths
1. knowing right from wrong
2. knowing consequences of actions
3. knowing various mental inclinations
4. knowing various mental faculties
5. knowing various degrees of intelligence
6. knowing the path to all goals
7. knowing ever-afflicted and purified phenomena
8. knowing past lives
9. knowing deaths and births
10. knowing the exhaustion of continuations

virtues
1. refraining from killing, and preserving life
2. refraining from stealing, and practicing generosity
3. refraining from sexual misconduct, and practicing moral ethics
4. refraining from lying, and speaking truthfully
5. refraining from divisive speech, and speaking harmoniously
6. refraining from harsh words, and speaking peacefully and politely
7. refraining from idle talk, and speaking meaningfully

8. refraining from covetousness, and practicing contentment
9. refraining from malice, and practicing loving-kindness and compassion
10. refraining from holding wrong views, and practicing the perfect meaning

Twelve

ayatana (sense spheres)

(sense organs)

1. eye
2. ear
3. nose
4. tongue
5. body
6. mind

(sense objects)

7. forms
8. sounds
9. odors
10. tastes
11. tangible objects
12. mental phenomena

deeds of the Buddha

1. descent from Tushita, the Joyous pure land
2. entering his mother's womb
3. taking birth
4. becoming skilled in various arts
5. delighting in the company of royal consorts
6. developing renunciation and becoming ordained
7. practicing austerities for six years

8. proceeding to the foot of the Bodhi Tree
9. overcoming Mara
10. becoming fully enlightened
11. turning the wheel of Dharma
12. passing into parinirvana

links of interdependence
1. ignorance
2. karmic formation
3. consciousness
4. name and form
5. six sense organs
6. contact
7. feeling
8. craving
9. grasping
10. becoming
11. rebirth
12. aging and death

Eighteen
dhatus (*elements*)
(the sense organs)
1. eye
2. ear
3. nose
4. tongue
5. body
6. mind
(the sense objects)
7. forms

8. sounds

9. odors

10. tastes

11. tangible objects

12. mental phenomena

(the sensory consciousnesses)

13. visual consciousness

14. auditory consciousness

15. olfactory consciousness

16. gustatory consciousness

17. tactile consciousness

18. mental consciousness

qualities of leisure and endowment. See *eight leisures; ten endowments.*

unshared or unique qualities of a buddha
1. A buddha is never confused.
2. A buddha does not engage in idle talk.
3. A buddha never forgets.
4. A buddha never loses meditative equipoise.
5. A buddha does not have any cognition of distinctness.
6. A buddha does not have nonanalytical equanimity.
7. A buddha's motivation never degenerates.
8. A buddha's perseverance never degenerates.
9. A buddha's mindfulness never degenerates.
10. A buddha's meditative concentration never degenerates.
11. A buddha's wisdom never degenerates.
12. A buddha's complete liberation never degenerates.
13. A buddha's every action of the body is preceded by wisdom and followed by wisdom.

14. A buddha's every action of speech is preceded by wisdom and followed by wisdom.
15. A buddha's every action of mind is preceded by wisdom and followed by wisdom.
16. A buddha sees the past through wisdom that is unattached and unobstructed.
17. A buddha sees the future through wisdom that is unattached and unobstructed.
18. A buddha sees the present through wisdom that is unattached and unobstructed.

Thirty-two

major marks of a buddha

1. The palms of his hands and soles of his feet bear signs of a wheel.
2. His feet are well set upon the ground like a tortoise.
3. His fingers and toes are webbed.
4. The palms of his hands and soles of his feet are smooth and tender.
5. His body has seven prominent features: broad heels, broad hands, broad shoulder blades, and a broad neck.
6. His fingers are long.
7. His heels are soft.
8. He is tall and straight.
9. His ankle bones do not protrude.
10. The hairs on his body point upward.
11. His ankles are like those of an antelope.
12. His hands are long and beautiful.
13. His male organ is withdrawn.
14. His body is the color of gold.
15. His skin is thin and smooth.

16. Each hair curls to the right.

17. His face is adorned by a coiled hair between his eyebrows.

18. The upper part of his body is like that of a lion.

19. His head and shoulders are perfectly round.

20. His shoulders are broad.

21. He has an excellent sense of taste, even of the worst tastes.

22. His body has the proportions of a banyan tree.

23. He has a protrusion on the crown of his head.

24. His tongue is long and thin.

25. His voice is mellifluent.

26. His cheeks are like those of a lion.

27. His teeth are white.

28. There are no gaps between his teeth.

29. His teeth are evenly set.

30. He has a total of forty teeth.

31. His eyes are the color of sapphire.

32. His eyelashes are like those of a magnificent heifer.

Thirty-seven
factors conducive to enlightenment
(the four mindfulnesses)
1. mindfulness of the body as impermanent and subject to decay
2. mindfulness of feelings—joy, suffering, and neutral feelings—as being transitory
3. mindfulness of mind as being like a cloud
4. mindfulness of phenomena as being interdependent
(the four abandonments)
5. abandoning nonvirtuous actions that had been taken up
6. not developing new nonvirtues
7. adopting new virtues that had not previously arisen

8. perfecting virtues that have arisen
(the four foundations of miracle powers)
9. absorption of aspiration
10. absorption of perseverance
11. absorption of meditation
12. absorption of analysis
(the five powers)
13. faith
14. perseverance
15. mindfulness
16. absorption
17. wisdom awareness
(the five strengths)
18. faith
19. perseverance
20. mindfulness
21. absorption
22. wisdom awareness
(the seven branches of enlightenment)
23. perfect mindfulness
24. perfect discrimination
25. perfect perseverance
26. perfect joy
27. perfect relaxation
28. perfect absorption
29. perfect equanimity
(the eightfold path)
30. perfect view
31. perfect conception
32. perfect speech
33. perfect action

34. perfect livelihood
35. perfect effort
36. perfect mindfulness
37. perfect absorption

Sixty
qualities of a buddha's melodious speech
1. gentle
2. soft
3. appealing
4. attractive
5. pure
6. flawless
7. distinct
8. captivating
9. worthy
10. indomitable
11. pleasant
12. melodious
13. clear
14. not rough
15. not coarse
16. extremely pleasing to hear
17. satisfying for body
18. satisfying for mind
19. delightful
20. creating happiness
21. without sorrow
22. instigating insight
23. comprehensible
24. elucidating

25. generating joy
26. utterly enjoyable
27. bringing comprehension
28. bringing full understanding
29. reasonable
30. relevant
31. free from the fault of repetition
32. melodious like the sound of the lion
33. melodious like the sound of the elephant
34. melodious like the sound of the dragon
35. melodious like the naga king
36. melodious like the gandharvas
37. melodious like the kalapinga bird
38. melodious like the voice of Brahma
39. melodious like the shangshang bird
40. majestic like the voice of Indra
41. majestic like the drum of Indra
42. not boastful
43. pervading all sounds without utterance
44. without corruption of words
45. without incompleteness
46. not feeble
47. not weak
48. extremely magnificent
49. pervasive
50. free from rigidity
51. connecting interruption
52. perfecting all sounds
53. satisfying the senses
54. not inferior
55. unchanging

56. not blurting
57. fully resounding to the assembly
58. endowed with the supreme of all aspects
59. teaches in the manner of the profound teachings
60. teaches in the manner of the vast teachings

Eighty

minor marks of a buddha

1. His nails are copper-colored.
2. His nails are moderately shiny.
3. His nails are raised.
4. His nails are round.
5. His nails are broad.
6. His nails are tapered.
7. His veins do not protrude.
8. His veins are free of knots.
9. His ankles do not protrude.
10. His feet are not uneven.
11. He walks with a lion's gait.
12. He walks with an elephant's gait.
13. He walks with a goose's gait.
14. He walks with a bull's gait.
15. His gait tends to the right.
16. His gait is elegant.
17. His gait is steady.
18. His body is well covered.
19. His body looks as if it were polished.
20. His body is well proportioned.
21. His body is clean and pure.
22. His body is smooth.
23. His body is perfect.

24. His sex organs are fully developed.

25. His physical bearing is excellent and dignified.

26. His steps are even.

27. His eyes are perfect.

28. He is youthful.

29. His body is not sunken.

30. His body is broad.

31. His body is not loose.

32. His limbs are well proportioned.

33. His vision is clear and unblurred.

34. His belly is round.

35. His belly is perfectly moderate.

36. His belly is not long.

37. His belly does not bulge.

38. His navel is deep.

39. His navel winds to the right.

40. He is perfectly handsome.

41. His habits are clean.

42. His body is free of moles and discoloration.

43. His hands are soft as cotton wool.

44. The lines of his palms are clear.

45. The lines of his palms are deep.

46. The lines of his palms are long.

47. His face is not too long.

48. His lips are red like copper.

49. His tongue is pliant.

50. His tongue is thin.

51. His tongue is red.

52. His voice is like thunder.

53. His voice is sweet and gentle.

54. His teeth are round.

55. His teeth are sharp.

56. His teeth are white.

57. His teeth are even.

58. His teeth are tapered.

59. His nose is prominent.

60. His nose is clean.

61. His eyes are clear.

62. His eyelashes are thick.

63. The black and white parts of his eyes are well defined and are like lotus petals.

64. His eyebrows are long.

65. His eyebrows are smooth.

66. His eyebrows are soft.

67. His eyebrows are evenly haired.

68. His hands are long and extended.

69. His ears are of equal size.

70. He has perfect hearing.

71. His forehead is well formed and well defined.

72. His forehead is broad.

73. His head is very large.

74. His hair is black as a bumble bee.

75. His hair is thick.

76. His hair is soft.

77. His hair is untangled.

78. His hair is not unruly.

79. His hair is fragrant.

80. His hands and feet are marked with auspicious emblems such as the shrivatsa and swastika.

Glossary of Names and Terms

action bodhichitta. Taking action to accomplish the goal of achieving enlightenment for the benefit of others; practicing the six perfections is the primary means of putting one's aspiration into action.

Ajatashatru (ca. fourth century BCE). He conspired with Devadatta to injure the Buddha and depose Ajatashatru's father, King Bimbisara. Later in life, he became a follower and patron of the Buddha.

Ananda (ca. fourth century BCE). Cousin and personal attendant of Shakyamuni Buddha. He is noted for having memorized all the Buddha's teachings verbatim and having recited them at the First Council. He was instrumental in the establishment of the ordination of women.

arhat. The culmination of the shravaka's path, it refers to one who is liberated from samsara but not fully enlightened. Nonetheless, they are accorded great respect within the Mahayana.

Asanga (ca. fourth century). An Indian master who is most remembered for having received five celebrated texts from Arya Maitreya—*Ornament of Clear Realization* (*Abhisamaya-lankara*), *Ornament of the Mahayana Sutras* (*Mahayanasutralamkara*), *Distinguishing the Middle from the Extremes*

(*Madhyantavibhaga*), *Distinguishing Dharma and Dhar-mata* (*Dharmadharmatvibhaga*), *Treatise on the Unsurpassed Tantra* (*Uttaratantra Shastra*)—for being the teacher and brother of Vasubandhu, and for founding the Yogacara school.

aspirational bodhichitta. A contemplation on the desire to achieve complete buddhahood.

Atisha (982–1055). After the suppression of Buddhism by King Langdarma, King Yeshé Öd invited Atisha to revive Buddhism in Tibet. Atisha was well-known in India, and spent twelve years studying bodhichitta in Sumatra. Atisha is the author of the *Lamp for the Path to Enlightenment* (*Bodhipathapradipa*).

Avalokiteshvara. A bodhisattva who most prominently embodies the quality of compassion. His is the most famous of all mantras: OM MANI PADME HUM.

bhikshu. A fully ordained monk.

bhumi. The literal meaning is stage, level, or ground. It refers to the progressive levels of a bodhisattva's training, each one of which successively provides the foundation for the next.

bodhichitta. The intention to achieve perfect, complete enlightenment for others' benefit. It is commonly categorized as relative or ultimate, with relative being further subdivided into aspirational and action (see separate entries).

buddha. One who has attained unsurpassable, complete, perfect enlightenment, i.e., one who has fully awakened all wisdom and fully purified all obscurations. Capitalized, "the Buddha" refers to Buddha Shakyamuni.

Devadatta (ca. fourth century BCE). Cousin of Buddha Shakyamuni. Once a monk under the Buddha, he created a schism in the sangha by attracting five hundred monks to a more ascetic lifestyle. He plotted with Ajatashatru to injure the Buddha, but was unsuccessful.

Dharma. This term has varied meanings depending on the context. When capitalized in this text, it refers to the holy teachings of the Buddha. When uncapitalized, it is a collective reference to all phenomena, i.e., things that have identifiable characteristics.

dharmakaya. One of the forms of a buddha. It denotes the ultimate nature of a buddha's wisdom form, which is nonconceptual and undefinable.

Dharmakirti (ca. seventh century). An Indian master from Nalanda University who was associated with the Yogacara school. He is most known for being a logician. His largest and most important work is the *Commentary on Valid Cognition* (*Pramanavarttika*).

empowerment. The tantric ritual by which one is empowered to perform a specific meditation practice, also called initiation.

Gampopa (1074–1153). Renowned as one of Tibet's greatest teachers, he is one of the foremost figures in the Kagyü lineage. His writings include *The Jewel Ornament of Liberation* and *A Precious Garland of the Supreme Path*.

initiation. See empowerment.

Jigten Sumgön (1143–1217). Founder of the Drigung Kagyü tradition. He was the heart-son of Phagmo Drupa, and widely recognized as an incarnation of Nagarjuna. His most famous writings include *One Thought* (Tibetan: *Gongchik*) and *Essence of the Mahayana Teachings* (Tibetan: *Ten Nying*).

Kagyü. One of the four principal traditions within Tibetan Buddhism, along with the Nyingma, Sakya, and Geluk schools; it originated with Buddha Vajradhara and was primarily transmitted by Tilopa and Naropa in India, and Marpa, Milarepa, and Gampopa in Tibet. It holds mahamudra and the six Dharmas of Naropa as its central teachings.

kalpa. Generically, an eon or other nearly limitless length of time. In Buddhist cosmology, it has the specific meaning of a complete cycle of a universe (a *mahakalpa*, or "great" kalpa) consisting of four stages: emptiness, formation, maintenance, and destruction.

karma. Physical, verbal or mental acts that imprint habitual tendencies in the mind. Upon meeting with suitable conditions, these habits ripen and become manifest in future events.

King Ashoka (late fourth or early third century BCE). A Mauryan emperor remembered for promoting Buddhist values and erecting inscribed pillars throughout his vast empire, and for installing memorials that marked events in the Buddha's life.

King Bimbisara (late fifth century BCE): The king of Magadha in ancient India, he was a great patron and follower of the Buddha.

liberation. Freedom from the suffering of samsara.

Mahakala. A fearsome-appearing protector deity.

mahamudra. The highest, most conclusive view that unites bliss and emptiness into one, the primordial effulgent nature of mind, and the ultimate realization of all phenomena of samsara and nirvana as they actually are. Its practice reveals the practitioner's basic, pure nature and leads to the experience of highest enlightenment.

Mara. Any negative influence that obstructs spiritual development, frequently personified as a demon-like being named Mara.

Meru. In Buddhist cosmology, a mountain that constitutes the center of the universe. It is surrounded by oceans and four principal continents.

Milarepa (1052–1135). One of the great masters of the Kagyü lineage, he is often referred to as an example of someone who attained enlightenment in a single lifetime. His vajra songs contain great healing qualities. He was Gampopa's primary teacher.

Nagarjuna (ca. second century). An Indian master of such critical importance to the propagation of the Mahayana that he is often called the "second Buddha." He founded the Madhyamaka philosophical school, which systematized the prajnaparamita (perfection of wisdom) teachings, and composed many texts that remain authoritative to the present day.

Naropa (1016–1100). One of the founding masters of the Kagyü tradition. He was a leading scholar at Nalanda University in India, which he renounced to become a yogi-practitioner under Tilopa. He is most remembered for being Marpa's teacher and for being the propagator of the teachings known as the six Dharmas of Naropa.

nirmanakaya. The physical form of a buddha purposefully manifested for the benefit of sentient beings. This is not necessarily a human form; they can appear as whatever is necessary.

nirvana. The unconfused state without suffering; the transcendence of samsara; sometimes called the complete, perfect, or nonabiding nirvana. *See also* partial nirvana.

outflow. That which flows out from the six sense organs; i.e., earthly desires, illusions, or defilements.

parinirvana. The final act of a fully enlightened buddha's life among humans or, in general, the death of any fully enlightened person.

partial nirvana. Stages of enlightenment experienced by hearers, solitary realizers, and bodhisattvas before they reach final nirvana or full enlightenment.

Phagmo Drupa (1110–70). A Tibetan lineage master of the Kagyü school, he was a student of Gampopa and teacher of Jigten Sumgön. His work *Engaging by Stages in the Teachings of the Buddha* (Tibetan: *Tenpa la rim gyu jukpai go*) has been translated into English.

prajna. Direct insight into transcendent knowledge, a faculty required to attain enlightenment.

pratyekabuddha. A self-liberated buddha whose attainment is less than the ultimate buddhahood. While they receive Dharma teachings at some point, they do not attain realization until after the Buddha's teachings have disappeared. Being without bodhichitta, they do not reach full enlightenment, but they do display miraculous powers to inspire devotion.

rains retreat. An annual monastic retreat lasting approximately three months and timed to coincide with the monsoon season.

relative bodhichitta. The mind that has vowed to accomplish full enlightenment in order to liberate all sentient beings from suffering. It can be aspirational or active.

samadhi. A profound meditative absorption in which the mind rests in the state free from conceptual thoughts.

sambhogakaya. A nonsubstantial, yet visible, body of a buddha or other great being, manifested to directly benefit bodhi-sattvas at high stages of realization and to serve as objects of devotion for practitioners.

samsara. The beginningless and endless cycle of rebirth throughout the six realms; the confused state of suffering from which Buddhists seek liberation.

sangha. Generally, the community of Buddhist practitioners. In different contexts, it can refer specifically to a monastic community or to an assembly of highly realized beings (arhats and bodhisattvas at the first bhumi and above).

Shavaripa (ca. eighth century). One of the eighty-four mahasid-dhas, he is a key figure in the transmission of the maha-mudra teachings.

sentient being. A conscious creature who is reborn within the six realms.

Shantideva (seventh–eighth century). An Indian master from Nalanda University most remembered as the author of *Engaging in the Bodhisattva's Way of Life* (*Bodhicharyavatara*) and the *Collection of Transcendent Instructions* (*Shiksasamuc-caya*). To this day, *Engaging in the Bodhisattva's Way of Life* is one of the most revered and widely read texts in the Maha-yana literature.

Shariputra (ca. fifth century BCE). One of Buddha Shakyamu-ni's two closest disciples, he is generally depicted as stand-ing to the Buddha's right. He was particularly distinguished by his wisdom.

shila. Appropriate conduct or moral ethics. It is the first of the three trainings and the second of the six perfections.

shravaka. A Hinayana disciple who hears the words of the Bud-dha's teachings, shares them with others, and aspires to become an arhat for his or her own benefit.

skandha. The collection of characteristics that constitutes a sentient being, often translated as "aggregates." Like a heap of grain, a being appears to be a single entity until, upon closer examination, it is understood to be comprised of many pieces.

svabhavikakaya. The underlying indivisible essence of all enlightened forms.

tathagata. An epithet for a buddha that refers to suchness, the pure essence of reality.

ultimate bodhichitta. A state of realization that is emptiness endowed with compassion that arises at the first bodhisattva bhumi.

Vajradhara. The primordial, dharmakaya buddha. He is often depicted as being a deep blue color to symbolizes his limitless qualities—infinite as the blue sky, fresh and clear after a rainfall when there are no clouds or dust to obscure its profundity.

vajrasana. The seat on which the Buddha reached enlightenment under the Bodhi Tree. It is considered to be the center of the universe and the place where all the buddhas of this fortunate eon reach enlightenment.

Vajrayana. The diamond path or "vehicle" of Buddhist tantra.

yidam. A deity whose form and attributes embody a particular aspect of enlightenment and with whom a practitioner identifies in meditation.

Notes

1. Shakyamuni Buddha, *The Dhammapada*, translated by Narada Thera (Colombo: B. M. S. Publication, 1978), 140.
2. From a vajra song by Jigten Sumgön, source unknown.
3. Translations of the *Heart Sutra* in this chapter are from The Dalai Lama, *Essence of the Heart Sutra: The Dalai Lama's Heart of Wisdom Teachings*, translated and edited by Thupten Jinpa (Boston: Wisdom Publications, 2005), 59–61.
4. Quoted in The Dalai Lama, *The World of Tibetan Buddhism: An Overview of Its Philosophy and Practice*, translated and edited by Thupten Jinpa (Boston: Wisdom Publications, 1995), 26.
5. *Bodhicharyavatara*, 3.23–24.
6. *Bodhicharyavatara*, 10.55.
7. *Nagarjuna's Letter to a Friend with Commentary by Kangyur Rinpoche*, trans. Padmakara Translation Group (Ithaca, NY: Snow Lion Publications, 2005), 29.
8. Quoted in Thuken Losang Chökyi Nyima, *The Crystal Mirror of Philosophical Systems*, translated by Geshé Lhundub Sopa (Somerville, MA: Wisdom Publications, 2009), 147.
9. Mark Siderits and Shoryu Katsura, *Nagarjuna's Middle Way: Mulamadhyamakakarika* (Somerville, MA: Wisdom Publications, 2013), 302.
10. Translated in The Dalai Lama, *Essence of the Heart Sutra: The Dalai Lama's Heart of Wisdom Teachings*, trans. and ed. Thupten Jinpa (Boston: Wisdom Publications, 2005), 59–61. Reprinted with permission from Wisdom Publications.

Annotated Bibliography

Bodhicharyavatara (*Engaging in the Bodhisattva's Way of Life*)
A beautiful presentation of the bodhisattva's training in verse form by the Indian master Shantideva. It is one of the most widely read and quoted of all Mahayana texts.

Śāntideva. *A Guide to the Bodhisattva Way of Life*. Translated by Vesna Wallace and B. Alan Wallace. Ithaca: Snow Lion, 1997.

Shantideva. *A Guide to the Bodhisattva's Way of Life*. Translated by Stephen Batchelor. Dharamsala: Library of Tibetan Works and Archives, 1979.

———. *The Bodhicaryāvatara*. Translated by Kate Crosby and Andrew Skilton. Oxford: Oxford University Press, 1996.

———. *Entering the Path of Enlightenment*. Translated by Marion L. Matics. New York: MacMillan, 1970.

———. *The Way of the Bodhisattva*. Translated by the Padmakara Translation Group. Boston: Shambhala Publications, 1997.

Sharma, Parmananda, trans. *Shantideva's Bodhicharyavatara*. New Delhi: Aditya Prakashan, 1990.

Buddhacarita (*Acts of the Buddha*)
An early Sanskrit poem attributed to Ashvaghosha relating the life story of the Buddha. Epigraphs in this book are translations by E. H. Johnston: chapter 1 (pp. 199–200), chapter 2 (p. 213), chapter 3 (p. 141), chapter 4 (pp. 60–62), chapter 6 (pp. 95–96), chapter 7 (pp. 182–85), chapter 8 (p. 3 and p. 10), and chapter 10 (pp. 2–3).

Asvaghosha. *Buddhacarita or Acts of the Buddha*. Translated by E. H. Johnston. Lahore: University of the Panjab, 1936. Reprint, Delhi: Motilal Banarsidass, 2015.

Asvaghosha. *The Buddhacarita or the Life of Buddha*. Edited and translated by Edward Cowell. 1894. Reprint. Independently published, 2017.

———. *Buddhacarita: Acts of the Buddha*. Translated by E. B. Cowell and edited by F. Max Muller. CreateSpace Publishing, 2015.

———. *Life of the Buddha*. Translated by Patrick Olivelle. New York: Clay Sanskrit Library, 2008.

———. *Buddhacarita: In Praise of Buddha's Acts*. Translated by Charles Willemen. Moranga, CA: BDK America, 2010.

Mulamadhyamakakarika (*Fundamental Verses of the Middle Way*)
The central text by Nagarjuna explaining the doctrines of emptiness and relative reality.

Garfield, Jay. *The Fundamental Wisdom of the Middle Way: Nāgārjuna's Mūlamadhyamakakārikā*. Oxford: Oxford University Press, 1995.

Inada, Kenneth. *Nāgārjuna: A Translation of his Mūlamadhyamakakārikā*. Tokyo: The Hokuseido Press, 1970.

Kalupahana, David. *Nāgārjuna: The Philosophy of the Middle Way*. Albany: State University of New York Press, 1986.

Nagarjuna. *The Root Stanzas of the Middle Way*. Translated by Padmakara Translation Group. Boulder: Shambhala, 2016.

Siderits, Mark, and Shoryu Katsura. *Nāgārjuna's Middle Way: Mūlamadhyamakakārikā*. Somerville, MA: Wisdom Publications, 2013.

Ganges Mahamudra
The great master Tilopa is said to have given these teachings to his disciple Naropa on the banks of the Ganges River. They comprise a short text on mahamudra, which has been widely taught for a millennium.

Rinjen Dorje, Garmapa. *The Vow and Aspiration of Mahamudra: Including the Pith Instructions of Mahamudra by Tilopa*. Translated by C. A. Muses and edited by Marilynn Hughes. CreateSpace Publishing, 2015.

Nyenpa, Sangyes. *Tilopa's Mahamudra Upadesha: The Gangama Instructions with Commentary*. Translated by David Molk. Boulder: Snow Lion Publications, 2014.

Thrangu, Khenchen. *Tilopa's Wisdom: His Life and Teachings on the Ganges Mahamudra*. Boulder: Snow Lion, 2019.

Gongchik (One Thought)
A concise presentation of the oral instructions of the Drigung Kagyü lineage that explains the unified, enlightened intention that is a common thread in all the teachings of the Buddha. Usually divided into seven chapters, it consists of vajra statements that were spoken by Jigten Sumgön and recorded by his disciple Chenga Sherab Jungné.

Samdup Rinpoche, Khenpo. *Clarifying the Central Thoughts of the Single Intention: A Commentary on Jigten Sumgön's Gongchig*. Translated by Mark Riege. Dayton, OH: Gar Drolma Buddhist Center, 2014.

Sumgon, Jigten. *Gongchig: The Single Intent, the Sacred Dharma*. Translated by Markus Viehbeck. Munich: Otter Verlag, 2009.

Sobisch, Jan-Ulrich. *The Buddha's Single Intention: Drigung Kyobpa Jikten Sumgön's Vajra Statements of the Early Kagyü Tradition*. Somerville, MA: Wisdom Publications, 2020.

Tsultrim Tenzin, Khenpo and Khenmo K. Trinlay Chodron. *Gong Chig: The Essence of the Profound View of the Dakpo Kagyu, A Wish-fulfilling Vase*. Frederick, MD: Tibetan Meditation Center, 2023.

The Great Kagyü Masters: The Golden Lineage Treasury
Translation of a thirteenth-century text that gathers the life stories of the founders of the Kagyü lineage together in one volume. It is very helpful to practitioners to have these accounts available for inspiration and guidance.

Gyaltsen, Khenpo Konchog. *The Great Kagyu Masters*. Boulder: Snow Lion Publications, 2006.

Mahaparinibbana Sutra
An early account of the end of the Buddha's life. Quotation on frontispiece from Walshe, pp. 263–64. Epigraph to chapter 9 from Rhys Davids, p. 114.

T. W. Rhys Davids, trans. *Buddhist Suttas*. The Sacred Books of the East. Vol. 11. Oxford: The Clarendon Press, 1881.

Walshe, Maurice. *The Long Discourses of the Buddha: A Translation of the Digha Nikaya*. Boston: Wisdom Publications, 1995.

Mahayanasutralamkara (*Ornament of the Mahayana Sutras*)
One of the five treatises by Maitreya that were transmitted through Asanga. It covers a broad range of topics within the Mahayana teachings.

Limaye, Surekha Vijay. *Mahayanasutralamkara by Asanga.* Delhi: Sri Satguru Publications, 1992.

Thurman, Robert, and Lobsang Jamspal, trans. *The Universal Vehicle Discourse Literature: Mahāyānasutrālaṃkāra.* New York: American Institute of Buddhist Studies, 2004.

Opening the Treasure of the Profound
Translation of songs of realization by Milarepa and Jigten Sumgön with commentary that explains them in contemporary terms.

Gyaltshen, Khenchen Konchog. *Opening the Treasure of the Profound.* Boulder: Snow Lion, 2013.

Scintillation of the Precious Vajra
The authoritative biography of Jigten Sumgön, written by his nephew and disciple.

Sherab Jungne, Chenga. *Scintillation of the Precious Vajra.* Munich: Otter Verlag, 2017.

The Gospel of Buddha
An early English retelling of the Buddha's life and teachings written to introduce and popularize Buddhism in the West. Epigraph to chapter 11 is from pp. 71–72.

Carus, Paul. *The Gospel of Buddha.* Chicago: The Open Court Publishing Company, 1894.

The History of Buddhism in India
Translation of a famous history written in the early 1600s by a renowned Tibetan scholar. Epigraph to chapter 5 is from p. 101.

Taranatha. *Taranatha's History of Buddhism in India.* Translated by Lama Chimpa and Alaka Chattopadhyayya. Delhi: Motilal Banarsidass, 2017.

Uttaratantra Shastra
One of the five texts transmitted by Maitreya to Asanga. The seminal work on buddha nature, it describes the nature and qualities of buddhahood.

Maitreya, Arya. *Buddha Nature: The Mahayana Uttaratantra Shastra with Commentary.* Commentary by Jamgön Kongtrül Lodrö Tayé and Khenpo Tsultrim Gyamtso Rinpoche. Translated by Rosemarie Fuchs. Boulder: Snow Lion, 2018.

Maitreya, Arya, and Acarya Asanga. *The Changeless Nature: Mahayana Uttara Tantra Shastra.* Translated by Ken and Katia Holmes. Eskdalemuir, Scotland: Karma Kagyu Trust, 1985.

Illustration Credits

About the Author

THE VILLAGE of Tsari and the surrounding areas are among the most sacred places in Tibet. It was there that Khenchen Rinpoche, Konchog Gyaltshen, was born in the spring of 1946, and it was there that he spent his early years. In 1960, because of the political situation in Tibet, Khenchen Rinpoche fled to India with his family. The family then settled in Darjeeling, where he began his education. Even at a young age, he was an excellent and dedicated student, and was able to complete his middle school studies in less than the average time.

At about this same time, a new university, the Central Institute of Higher Tibetan Studies, opened in Varanasi, India. Determined to be among its first students, Khenchen Rinpoche traveled to Varanasi in October 1967 to seek admission. He then began a nine-year course of study that included Madhyamaka, Abhidharma, Vinaya, the *Abhisamayalankara*, and the *Uttaratantra*, as well as history, logic, and Tibetan grammar. In early 1968, he had the good fortune to take full monastic ordination from the great Kalu Rinpoche and, shortly after graduating from the Institute, he received teachings from the Sixteenth Gyalwa Karmapa on *The Eight Treasures of Mahamudra Songs* by the Indian mahasiddhas.

Even after completing this long and arduous course of study, Khenchen Rinpoche wanted only to deepen his knowledge and practice of the Dharma. With the same intensity that he brought to his earlier studies, Rinpoche sought out and received teachings and instructions from great Buddhist masters. One was the Venerable Khunu Lama Rinpoche, with whom Khenchen Rinpoche studied two works of Gampopa— *The Jewel Ornament of Liberation* and *A Precious Garland of the Excellent Path*. His studies with the Venerable Khunu Lama also included Mahamudra and many of the songs of Milarepa.

Maintaining a balance between theoretical understanding and the practice of meditation, Khenchen Rinpoche began a three-year retreat in 1978 under the guidance of the enlightened master Khyunga Rinpoche. During this time, he was able to deepen and enhance his understanding of *The Fivefold Path of Mahamudra* and the profound *One Thought* of Lord Jigten Sumgön. He also received many other transmissions.

In 1985, Khenchen Rinpoche traveled to the main seat of the Drigung Kagyü lineage, Drigung Thil, in Tibet. There, he was able to receive personal blessings, as well as instructions and transmissions of mahamudra and the six yogas of Naropa, from the enlightened master Venerable Pachung Rinpoche.

In 1982, the force of karma and the requests of many practitioners combined to bring Khenchen Rinpoche to the United States. By late 1983, the Tibetan Meditation Center was well established in Washington, D.C. Their original location was the site of innumerable teachings, practices, retreats, and ceremonies. In September 1984, and again in 1987, the young center was blessed with personal visits and teachings by His Holiness the Dalai Lama. Through Khenchen Rinpoche's and the center's efforts, Drikung Kyabgön Chetsang Rinpoche visited in

1987, 1994, and 1999, and people in several states were able to receive benefit from his teachings and presence.

With the Tibetan Meditation Center as his base, Khenchen Rinpoche went on to establish practice centers in Big Sur, CA; Boston, MA (currently under the direction of Lama Sonam); Boulder, CO; Chicago, IL (currently under the direction of Drupon Rinchen Dorjee); Gainesville, FL; Lidingö, Sweden; Los Angeles, CA; Madison, WI; Pittsburgh, PA; San Francisco, CA; Santiago, Chile (currently under the direction of Khenpo Phuntsok Tenzin); Tampa Bay, FL (currently under the direction of Drupon Thinley Ningpo); and Virginia Beach, VA; as well as Dharmakirti College in Tucson, AZ, and Vajra Publications.

Wanting the teachings of Dharma to reach as many people as possible, Khenchen Rinpoche has quickly adapted himself to Western forms of communication. He has made appearances on television, been a guest on many radio programs, lectured extensively at colleges and universities, and spoken to the public through countless newspaper articles. Between 1983 and 1990, Khenchen Rinpoche single-handedly translated critical Drigung Kagyü practices, prayers, and histories into English. Before Tibetan fonts were available for computers, he wrote them out by hand. Later, when automation became available, the translations were polished and republished. This priceless work formed the essential base from which the holy Dharma could be taught and practiced.

Khenchen Rinpoche and the Tibetan Meditation Center moved to Frederick, Maryland in November 1991. Nestled inside a state park, the Center is now situated on four wooded acres. A small temple and a stupa have been built there, and repeatedly consecrated by many esteemed lamas. With this larger facility and in surroundings more conducive to contemplation, Khenchen Rinpoche was able to benefit even more people with his teachings. In later years, he left the Center in the capable hands of Khenpo Tsultrim Tenzin.

Now in semi-retirement, Khenchen Rinpoche has taken the title of "Khensur," meaning something like Khenchen Emeritus. He lives quietly in Madison, WI (USA). He continues to translate and write, but has curtailed much of his travel. Remembering the struggles of his early years, Khenchen Rinpoche inspires and supports monks, nuns and lay people in their practice of the Dharma and is always ready to assist them in whatever way he can. To all, he gives of himself freely. With his heart and mind turned firmly toward the Dharma, he compassionately and patiently shows the way to liberation.

What to Read Next
from Wisdom Publications

Ornament of Dakpo Kagyü Thought
Short Commentary on the Mahāmudrā Aspiration Prayer
By Rangjung Dorjé and Mendong Tsampa Rinpoché
Translated by Sarah Harding

"Sarah Harding clarifies the essence of mahāmudrā with characteristic humor and penetrating insight, including points of contention. These pithy texts, elegantly translated, are contemplations on lucid awareness and immeasurable compassion, sparking illumination while refreshing one's language skills!" —Karma Lekshe Tsomo, professor of Buddhist Studies, University of San Diego

Mahāmudrā
A Practical Guide
His Eminence Zurmang Gharwang Rinpoche

"Gharwang Rinpoche's work serves as a definitive manual, guiding aspiring mahāmudrā students along the complete path, beginning with a clear presentation of the preliminaries, through a detailed presentation of śamatha and vipaśyanā, and concluding with enlightening instructions on the actualization of the result." —from the foreword by His Holiness the Sakya Trichen

About Wisdom Publications

Wisdom Publications is the leading publisher of classic and contemporary Buddhist books and practical works on mindfulness. To learn more about us or to explore our other books, please visit our website at wisdom.org or contact us at the address below.

Wisdom Publications
132 Perry Street
New York, NY 10014 USA

We are a 501(c)(3) organization, and donations in support of our mission are tax deductible.

Wisdom Publications is affiliated with the Foundation for the Preservation of the Mahayana Tradition (FPMT).